W9-CIG-432

WITHDRAWN

Passages to Literature

Passages to Literature

Essays on Teaching in Australia, Canada,
England, the United States, and Wales

Edited by

Joseph O'Beirne Milner
Wake Forest University

Lucy Floyd Morcock Milner
North Carolina Governor's School

National Council of Teachers of English
1111 Kenyon Road, Urbana, Illinois 61801

Staff Editor: Rona S. Smith

Book Design: Tom Kovacs for TGK Design

NCTE Stock Number 34998-3020

Library of Congress Cataloging in Publication Data

Passages to literature: essays on teaching in Australia, Canada, England, the
    United States, and Wales/edited by Joseph O'Beirne Milner, Lucy Floyd
    Morcock Milner.
        p.   cm.
    Includes bibliographies.
    ISBN 0-8141-3499-8
    1. English literature—Study and teaching (Secondary) I. Milner,
Joseph O'Beirne, 1937– . II. Milner, Lucy Floyd Morcock, 1941– . III.
National Council of Teachers of English.
PR37.P37   1989
807'.12—dc19   89-3172
                                                                      CIP

Contents

Preface

Passages to Literature: Essays on Teaching in Australia, Canada, England, the United States, and Wales was conceived in a rare but appropriate setting—a meeting of the International Federation of Teachers of English (IFTE). The setting was rare because the formal agenda of that meeting and of the paper one of us developed for it were devoted to the recent preoccupation with *writing* instruction rather than *literature* instruction. What became clear was that, despite the focus on writing, some very clever, serious, and profitable thinking was being directed toward new ways of approaching literature in our classrooms. Leaders in other English-speaking countries, new and old, were excited about the once dominant but now somewhat neglected area of literature instruction. As these informal talks progressed, we realized that what these people were saying about how literature should be taught was having a powerful effect on our understanding. We felt that these ideas might be equally engaging and enriching to other English teachers.

Thus conversation soon moved to a more formal request for papers from nine English teachers from Australia, Canada, England, Wales, and the United States—all respected practitioners in their own countries. We asked them simply to expound upon their latest thinking about literature instruction for middle school and secondary students. Their papers have become the chapters of this book.

The papers are unified in their energy, seriousness, and originality. They differ in their basic assumptions (most, though not all, are reader-response oriented), their scope (some are theoretical; some concretely delineate classroom questions, activities, evaluation), their student audience (most concentrate on secondary students; some treat middle-grade students), and their political compass (two seriously reckon with the political realities of their respective countries). Pervading all nine chapters are a profound respect for both reader and text and serious and diverse attempts to bring the two into creative collaboration. The last sentence of Probst's chapter nicely sums up this central idea: "Readers must come to respect both the text and themselves, and peer carefully into both if they are to read well and happily."

The first four chapters articulate the reader-response approach to literature espoused by Louise Rosenblatt. Robert Probst, Ken Watson, and John Dixon and Leslie Stratta present grounds for their belief in the importance of this approach, and they further suggest concrete methods for achieving this kind of active collaboration. Patrick Dias shows the need for aligning the evaluation process with the basic assumption of a reader-response approach, so that the latter is not altered or undermined by final school-leaving examinations.

After the theoretical and practical foundation provided by these four chapters, chapters 5 and 6 present a tacit demonstration of the reader-response approach, with two specific models for the classroom. Ben Brunwin and Peter Adams delineate two imaginative approaches to engaging students in fiction, both of which are designed to create levels of student involvement in the literature that are not always brought about by analytic, logical, formal exercises.

The final three chapters are less single-minded about the reader-response approach, although all manifest a basic faith in engaging students with the text. In the seventh chapter, Derrick Sharp argues for a combination of the best features of the reader-response and formal methods of teaching literature. In chapter 8, Joseph Milner delineates a developmental approach to teaching literature which has reader response as its fundamental and important first stage but incorporates three other, more analytical, critical and scholarly methods as well. Michael Cooke's chapter ends the collection with a broad look at literature instruction, drawn from a different perspective and with a broader brush, but fitting nevertheless. He calls for a redefinition of the humanities, a view which promotes personal freedom and creativity and, like the other authors, a sense of participating individually and socially in the human powers at work in literature.

American readers may be startled by some spelling and usage that depart from standard American English. We have tried to preserve the original language and standardize lesser things. More important, American readers may have a tendency to smile a bit when stories of what works in classrooms in England or other foreign places are brought up as models for change. The care, the rigor, the intellect of our English-speaking colleagues is deeply acknowledged by most of us, but as with the model of the British Infant School, American critics often reject these good ideas because of the cultural differences anticipated and encountered in transplanting them into the soil of American schools. The ideas contained within this book appear culture-proof. The literature is more often the same than different; the approaches, though new, are not unknown to or untested by American teachers; the goals for instruction are also similar. So the classroom experience, the pedagogical vision, the literary insights offered in these chapters should not be lost on us.

We need to widen our perspectives and open up these broader passages for consideration of what might be, what ought to be, the case in English classrooms. These passages should connect us with the shared venture of other English-speaking teachers engaged in considering how literature can best be taught. They admit us a bit into what George Eliot suggested was her aim: to discern "how ideas lie in other minds than my own." These practitioners do not claim to have discovered "the great revelation." Instead, to continue Virginia Woolf's metaphor, they represent for us, the editors, "little daily miracles, illuminations, matches struck unexpectedly in the dark." We trust they will provide similar light for you, the reader.

Joseph O'Beirne Milner
Lucy Floyd Morcock Milner

I Reader Response: Theory and Practice

1 The River and Its Banks: Response and Analysis in the Teaching of Literature

Robert E. Probst
Georgia State University
Atlanta, Georgia, United States

Passages to Literature opens with Robert Probst's chapter because it so lucidly presents the collection's basic respect for both reader and text. Probst believes that reading literature is not to be undertaken to find objective knowledge, but rather to make meaning in the interaction between the reader's unique personal experience and the text. Probst carefully delineates one approach to teaching literature that demonstrates the pedagogical implications of this interdependence: it accepts and respects an individual student's uniqueness, invites the student to be personally involved in the text, encourages a freedom of response, and uses the student's personal experience to shape reading.

> The mind fits the world and shapes it as a river fits and shapes its own banks.
>
> —Annie Dillard, *Living by Fiction*

The Uniqueness of Personal Knowledge

A colleague of mine and I used to argue in bars. We would fall to discussing the politics of the university or the significance of some public pronouncement on the state of education, and inevitably the moment would come when she would make a prediction or draw an inference that began with "I know that . . ." and we would be off. Gently, tactfully, professorially, I would ask, "How do you *know*?," seeking the evidence, the accumulation of fact, the chain of reasoning that would promote her statement from the dubious ranks of speculation and conjecture to the more dignified stature of knowledge.

"Well," she would say, "I just know," and she would offer what seemed to me a feeble assortment of further speculations and guess-

3

es in support of her assertion. "Perhaps you *believe*," I'd suggest. "Perhaps you *think* it to be the case, but it doesn't seem that you have enough evidence to claim that you *know*." She would never bend. When she felt that she knew, she would not relinquish that claim, regardless of the insubstantiality of her evidence. Ultimately, frustration winning out over patience, I'd pound on the table, shouting, "No! You don't *know*—you surmise, you guess, you intuit, speculate, hope, wish, suspect, infer, opine, gather, conjecture, fancy, hypothesize, imagine, presume, or deduce—you do *not* goddam well know!"

But she always did.

I came to realize that she was thinking about matters—especially those that had to do with the attitudes and behavior of people—in ways drastically different from, and much more effective than, mine. She focused on different elements and worked with them in different ways. While I cast aside as irrelevant and unreliable the vague and barely articulated feelings that intruded upon my efforts to analyze a situation, she would seize upon her own feelings—the vaguer and less fully articulated, the better—and somehow forge insight out of them.

There are, I began to realize, a great many elements in any situation, and from them we select only a few with which to deal. Furthermore, I decided, there are a variety of ways in which to handle information and experience, and we all have our preferred strategies. Although Western culture has deferred to Socrates and Bacon and insisted upon objectivity and rational analysis—in other words, upon a simulation of the scientific method—there remains an undeniable personal element in all thought. We do not manage to adhere rigorously to principles of rational inquiry, and it might not be desirable even if we could, for there seem to be other ways of dealing with information that work effectively. Thought remains the act of an individual, and thus it is idiosyncratic, a unique personal creation, no matter how much it may pretend to rigorous objectivity.

The Personal Significance of Literature

Literary thought is particularly idiosyncratic. The literary work, after all, is significant only insofar as it touches a reader's mind. As Rosenblatt has said, "A novel or poem or play remains merely inkspots on paper until a reader transforms them into a set of meaningful symbols" (1983, 25).

It is in the transforming act of reading that the inkspots become words, that the words come to act as symbols, and thus that ink and paper become poem or play. Individual readers enact this transformation upon the text, and they must do it with whatever resources at their command, in whatever way they are able. But they cannot, of course, be anything or anyone but themselves while reading, and thus the reading, the meaning made in the act of reading, is unique to each individual.

And that is as it should be. The substance of literature is human experience—the complex relationships in which people become involved, the emotions they suffer or enjoy, the experiences they encounter, the value and significance with which they vest one thing or another. Whatever readers may find in books about the great issues—love, death, justice, good and evil—they must somehow connect with their own experiences. Love in *Romeo and Juliet* must be understood through one's own experiences with the emotion, and the play will have significance or not for the reader insofar as the reader's experience makes it comprehensible and insofar as the play sheds light upon that experience. The reader must appropriate the text, not by slavishly submitting to it, attempting to do nothing but absorb it, but rather by both submitting and reflecting, by both accepting the visions offered in the text and testing them against his or her own and others. Objective scientific study may provide information about all of these matters, but what the individual values, feels, and makes of past experiences, literary and otherwise, must inevitably be something unique:

> [A]s human beings we must inevitably see the universe from a centre lying within ourselves and speak about it in terms of a human language shaped by the exigencies of human intercourse. Any attempt rigorously to eliminate our human perspective from our picture of the world must lead to absurdity. (Polanyi 1958, 3)

The individuality of the reader inevitably shapes the confrontation with experience of any kind. Whatever new experience one encounters must be dealt with on the basis of experiences already had. It is simply not intellectually possible to bypass or disregard what a reader brings to the new experience or the new text. Jauss (1982), in arguing for fuller attention in literary studies to the reception of the literary work by the reader, remarks,

> For even the critic who judges a new work, the writer who conceives of his work in light of positive or negative norms of an earlier work, and the literary historian who classifies a work in

its tradition and explains it historically are first simply readers
before their reflexive relationship to literature can become productive again. In the triangle of author, work, and public the
last is no passive part, no chain of mere reactions, but rather itself an energy formative of history. (19)

Even the professional, Jauss says, is at first simply a reader, and
even the nonprofessional reader, the public, the collective reader,
shapes history as the receiver of the literary work. Jauss's view denies that it is the writer alone who influences the course of events,
or that it is the critic and the literary historian, the professional
assessors of literature, who alone determine what the work's effects
will be, but that it is the ordinary person, as reader, who affects history. If that is the case, then we have reason to be concerned about
the ways in which readers confront texts. We would hope, presumably, to produce responsible—whatever that may mean to us—readers of literary texts.

Literature and the Making of Meaning

We are concerned here not so much with the role of the audience in
the making of history, in reshaping the norms of a society or a
culture, as with the possibility that an individual reader may form
his or her own history. If readers see the literary work as a significant comment on their own experiences, and as thought that might
be employed in reshaping their own visions, then they may assume
the more active, creative role Jauss suggests is appropriate and work
with the literature to forge their own knowledge.

For literature, as we have argued, is not knowledge ready-made,
but rather the material from which each individual must shape his
or her own knowledge. Literary knowledge is not something *found*
in a text, not something concealed within like a pearl in an oyster,
not something to be figured out, like a mystery or a riddle. Rather it
is something to be created in the acts of reading, discussing, and
writing about what has been read.

There is, between the book and the reader, a transaction, as Rosenblatt (1987) puts it, in which neither text nor reader has exclusive
control. Rosenblatt goes so far as to redefine *text* and *poem* so that
the printed page and its symbolic functioning will be clearly distinguished:

[I]n a reading situation "the text" may be thought of as the
printed signs in their capacity to serve as symbols.

> "Poem" presupposes a reader actively involved with a text and refers to what he makes of his responses to the particular set of verbal symbols. (12)

A poem, then, does not exist until the reader comes along and reads it, and, consequently, the meaning of the poem cannot exist except in the context of a reader reading.[1] Rosenblatt comments:

> The popular phrasing is: the reader "finds" the meanings in the text. This has at least the merit of rejecting the imposition of irrelevant meanings: the reader should not project ideas or attitudes that have no defensible linkage with the text. But one can with equal justice say that one "finds" the meanings for the verbal symbols in himself. Actually, both formulations are false: to find the meanings solely in the text or to find them solely in the reader's mind. The finding of meanings involves both the author's text and what the reader brings to it. (14)

Iser (1978) suggests a similar relationship between reader and text:

> [T]he literary work has two poles, which we might call the artistic and the aesthetic: the artistic pole is the author's text and the aesthetic is the realization accomplished by the reader. In view of this polarity, it is clear that the work itself cannot be identical with the text or with the concretization, but must be situated somewhere between the two. It must inevitably be virtual in character, as it cannot be reduced to the reality of the text or to the subjectivity of the reader, and it is from this virtuality that it derives its dynamism. As the reader passes through the various perspectives offered by the text and relates the different views and patterns to one another he sets the work in motion, and so sets himself in motion, too. (21)

And it is that "motion" that yields meaning:

> [W]e can say that literary texts initiate "performances" of meaning rather than actually formulating meanings themselves. (26–27)

The Reader's Situation

What is the situation, then, of a reader confronting a literary text? Each reader comes to the text with a background of experience and thought, out of which has been abstracted the information and the intellectual and emotional habits needed to make sense of the work. The sense that the reader does manage to make depends as much upon that background as it does upon the words on the page. The meaning of a literary work depends, then, upon the mind of the reader as much as it does upon the words on the page. If meaning is to emerge during the act of reading, it must be created by the reader—the student—and not the teacher or critic or commentator.

In the teaching of literature, perhaps more so than in any other discipline, we must recognize, as Polanyi said, that the center lies within. Students will see the literary work, not from the perspective of the scholar, or of the author, or of the teacher, but from their own perspective—they *cannot* see it in any other way. They cannot look at the text or the world through any eyes but their own. That is, obviously, a limited perspective, but it is also a unique perspective, one that no one else has, one that enables a student to contribute uniquely. And, since literature deals not with scientific, objective, generalizable data, but with the human encounter with the world, it is appropriate that the individual reader deal with his or her *own* perspective. After all, students are concerned with *their* unique connections with the world, *their* own experiences and thoughts rather than the typical or the average or the probable. We might hope that they would broaden their perspectives, come to understand more fully and see more clearly, but if this is to occur as a result of the reading, if an individual's vision is to be clarified and sharpened, it is nonetheless *that individual's* perspective and vision that are in question. A reader must begin with his or her own knowledge and ways of dealing with the world in order to develop new or modified knowledge and skill.

The reader and the text, then, are as mutually shaping as the river and its banks. They act upon one another, transact with one another, and the final shape of the poem depends not simply upon one or the other, but upon the joining of the two.

Teaching: Response and Analysis

What are the implications of this interdependence of the reader and the text for the teaching of literature? Clearly, the first is that the uniqueness of the individual student must be acknowledged, accepted, and respected. The student cannot be viewed simply as the passive recipient of information, but rather must be seen as the maker of his or her own knowledge. According to Bleich (1978), "the purpose of pedagogical institutions from the nursery through the university is to synthesize knowledge rather than to pass it along" (133). Students, regardless of age or ability, must do their own synthesizing—it cannot be done for them.

Instruction, consequently, must be planned to involve students in the act of making meaning—they cannot merely be presented with an accumulation of information about writer and text, nor can they be given, as final judgment, the considered opinions of the preeminent critics and scholars.

To do so is to burden students with undigested information and to imply that such information constitutes knowledge. Instead, students must be invited to confront the text, to respond to it in whatever way comes naturally, and to begin there the process of making knowledge.

And how might that be done? Consider one of the simple but effective strategies Bleich (1975) has recommended.[2] He suggests that students be asked to identify the most important word in a text they have read. From even a short poem, a group of students will choose a collection of words diverse enough to stimulate conversation about why a particular word seems important to one student and not to another, and about what constitutes importance.

The request to identify the most important word, by its very ambiguity, implies to students that they are free to decide for themselves, on the basis of their own criteria, whatever those criteria may be and whether they are articulated or not. The request invites students to consult their own thoughts and feelings. It is not the sort of question to which there is one correct—or even best—answer, and unless the teacher errs by insisting, in the course of the discussion, that there actually is one "most important" word, students should easily be able to see that the differences in their answers represent not errors or deviations or mistakes, but normal and respectable differences in perspective. And it is an awareness of those differences that is sought, rather than conformity to a prescribed interpretation or an established judgment.

So we begin by telling students that they are free to respond to the work in whatever way seems natural. They are free to confront the work honestly, prodded only by that one simple instruction: identify the most important word. Students are not asked at this point to consult critics or to produce a complex chain of reasoning. They are simply asked to make a quick judgment about what word seems or feels or looks important. And yet the question leads almost inevitably to analysis, both of the text and of the diverse readings of the text that may arise.

Students are likely to scrutinize the choices of others and to defend their own choices in several ways, the first and most obvious of which is through an appeal to the words on the page. Something in the text suggests to students the main idea, the most significant thought, and they identify the word that most fully represents that idea or theme. Consider several responses to the following poem by Louis Simpson:

My Father in the Night Commanding No

My father in the night commanding No
Has work to do. Smoke issues from his lips;
    He reads in silence.
The frogs are croaking and the streetlamps glow.

And then my mother winds the gramophone;
The Bride of Lammermoor begins to shriek—
    Or reads a story
About a prince, a castle, and a dragon.

The moon is glittering above the hill.
I stand before the gateposts of the King—
    So runs the story—
Of Thule, at midnight when the mice are still.

And I have been in Thule! It has come true—
The journey and the danger of the world,
    All that there is
To bear and to enjoy, endure and do.

Landscapes, seascapes . . . where have I been led?
The names of cities—Paris, Venice, Rome—
    Held out their arms.
A feathered god, seductive, went ahead.

Here is my house. Under a red rose tree
A child is swinging; another gravely plays.
    They are not surprised
That I am here; they were expecting me.

And yet my father sits and reads in silence,
My mother sheds a tear, the moon is still,
    And the dark wind
Is murmuring that nothing ever happens.

Beyond his jurisdiction as I move
Do I not prove him wrong? And yet, it's true
    They will not change
There, on the stage of terror and of love.

The actors in that playhouse always sit
In fixed positions—father, mother, child
    With painted eyes.
How sad it is to be a little puppet!

Their heads are wooden. And you once pretended
To understand them! Shake them as you will,
    They cannot speak.
Do what you will, the comedy is ended.

Father, why did you work? Why did you weep,
Mother? Was the story so important?
  "Listen!" the wind
Said to the children, and they fell asleep.

(*Man in the Poetic Mode*, 1970)

One student suggested that *silence* was the most important word, pointing out that much of the poem seemed to be about the isolation of the characters from one another. The mother is off in her story-land, the father is hidden in his paper, and the child is separated from them both. Their separateness was captured for the student most fully in the word *silence*. "No one," he observed, "talked to anyone else."

This student, and several others whose reactions were similar, elaborated upon the thought at some length, identifying aspects of the text that contributed to their impression and remarking upon patterns in their own lives as well. One observed that in his house, television played the role both of the mother's gramophone and of the father's newspaper—television was for his mother the source of fantasy and escape and for his father the source of entertainment or distraction from the day's work.

That student's observation is particularly interesting for several reasons. It demonstrates, first of all, how important personal experience is in shaping the reading of a text. To explain an element of the text, the student referred to his own experience—he found within himself the resources that enabled him to clarify the text. Second, it suggests how that personal experience might confound the issue. We might notice, for example, that the student has invented a detail that the poet has not given. The student sees the father not just reading, but reading a particular item, a newspaper, for distraction or entertainment, and yet Simpson says only that "he reads in silence," without telling us what he reads, and that he "has work to do," suggesting that the reading is not merely for pleasure. The student, in crafting his vision of the poem, has invented a detail that allows him to diminish the significance of the father's reading from "work" to "distraction." The student's observation also demonstrates how quickly and easily the discussion can move onto difficult ground. The student began to discuss private matters—the relationship within his own family—that could be awkward to handle and that might be considered inappropriate for the classroom. Clearly, a willingness to consider responses to literary works obligates a teacher to remain alert to the possibility that sensitive topics may come up and exposes the teacher to the possibility that he or she will be accused of trespassing upon the privacy of the students and their families. The teacher must be prepared to handle delicate matters with discretion, guarding prudently against inappropriate intrusions into private matters, and must be prepared as well to defend particular approaches to literary texts.

A second student, responding to the poem somewhat differently, suggested that *father* was the most important word. When asked why, he muttered something nebulous and evasive and declined to elaborate further, suggesting by his behavior that the poem had touched chords too troubling to deal with publicly. Discreetly, the teacher and the class moved on to deal with other reactions, allowing the student to reflect upon his concerns in solitude.

Clearly, there are similarities in the two responses. Each response arose, in part, from reflections upon the reader's experiences within his own family, and both students attended, more or less, to the text. For both students the text seemed to promote thought about private matters. Both seemed more interested in the issue raised by the poem—however they might wish to characterize it—than in other matters that might conceivably have been examined. They were not interested, for example—although other students were—in the elusive references to *The Bride of Lammermoor* or to Thule. In fact, the more talkative student seemed impatient with the desire expressed by others to have those allusions explained, considering their questions a time-wasting digression from more important matters. The more reticent student, though content to have the discussion move to less disturbing issues, seemed to consider the questions irrelevant and uninteresting.

Although both students were more interested in examining their own responses than in other possible approaches to the text, their behavior in the class was different, and each required a different reaction from the teacher. The first student, although he apparently wanted to contemplate personal matters, was not reluctant to discuss (at least some of) them with the class. The other student, also reflecting upon personal matters, was unwilling to talk them over with the group. And yet eventually, as they tried to make sense of their responses and perceptions, both found themselves led to closer readings of the text.

The first student was startled to discover that Simpson had *not* specified that it was a newspaper the father was reading. He had been certain that it was, and he reread the text carefully, fully expecting to find *newspaper* in there somewhere. When the word failed to appear, he began to realize that he had indeed insinuated something into the text, and that what he had invented revealed something about his own experience and how that might differ from the experience conjured by the poet.

He began to see, in other words, that the meaning he had distilled from the reading represented a coming-together of the text and his own experience, and he began to grow more observant of the intermingling of the two. After brief discussion, he was able to acknowledge that his experience with his own family was somewhat different from that presented in the text, and he began to articulate some of those dissimilarities. Doing so enabled him to see both the text and his own experience more clearly.

It is more difficult to see what was happening with the other reader, the quiet one, reluctant to talk about his reactions, but we may speculate that given the opportunity and the proper encouragement and support, he might profit from the reading. If the text did touch a resonant but perhaps painful chord, then the open forum of the classroom is not the place to deal with it. But it might be dealt with nonetheless in the privacy of a journal or in the intimacy of talks the student may seek out with friends or teachers he trusts. One of the virtues of literature is that it objectifies experience, allowing us to deal with intensely personal and difficult experience in a less menacing context. We can, if it suits us, speak of the isolation of the character in Simpson's poem, even if it is our own isolation that troubles us. We can exercise a control over the literary experience that we may not have elsewhere.

It is clear, however, that both students entered into the text through their own experiences. They looked at it first through the conceptual screens they had developed in their experiences with fathers, families, and other texts. The poems that each made of this particular text were shaped by all of that preceding experience. And it is evident, too, at least for the more loquacious student, that the poem made was also shaped by the text. He did not, ultimately, see in the text only what he had seen already in his own life, but rather came to see that the text offered a new experience, and thus he was able to broaden and modify his own perspective.

Bleich (1975) says, in observing the movement of one of his students away from personal matters toward broader social and political issues in the discussion of a literary work, that "it is a relatively common psychological habit of people to shift the discussion to such large terms when they sense that the time has come to dissolve the personal issue altogether . . ." (47). He remarks further that "the habit of objectification is fundamental in human mental functioning, and no one does without it. . . . There will come a point in almost anyone's response when some form of objectification will come to the rescue to depersonalize the response" (48).

But the study of literature cannot be completely depersonalized—to do so is to reduce it to insignificance and to deprive it of its power to inform and to touch the reader. If we ignore the primary connection between the reader and the text, or deny the importance of the reader's perceptions and responses, then we delude the reader about the act of reading and discourage him or her from accepting responsibility for the making of meaning.

The problem in teaching literature may be in encouraging a rational perspective on that process of moving between the personal and the impersonal, between responding and analyzing those responses. Patterns of instruction have, for a long time, deluded students into thinking that there was an objective reality to literary knowledge—that it was demonstrable and verifiable, primarily through reference to the text. To allow them to stray to the opposite pole, where they may insist that there is nothing beyond their own perceptions, their own assertions, would, of course, be equally deceitful and damaging. They need instead to learn that the knowledge emerging from the act of reading is like the shape of the river and its banks—neither the river nor the shore determines, in and of itself, what that shape will be. Rather, they work their effects upon each other, acting and responding, shaping and being shaped. Readers must come to respect both the text and themselves, and peer carefully into both if they are to read well and happily.

Notes

1. Rosenblatt continues by suggesting that the term "'poem' stands here for the whole category, 'literary work of art,' and for such terms as 'novel,' 'play,' or 'short story.' This substitution is often justified by the assertion that poems are the most concentrated form of the category, the others being more extended in time, more loosely integrated."

2. Bleich suggests a number of strategies in this useful book.

References

Bleich, David. 1975. *Readings and Feelings: An Introduction to Subjective Criticism.* Urbana, Ill.: National Council of Teachers of English.

Bleich, David. 1978. *Subjective Criticism.* Baltimore: Johns Hopkins University Press.

Iser, Wolfgang. 1978. *The Act of Reading: A Theory of Aesthetic Response*. Baltimore: Johns Hopkins University Press.

Jauss, Hans Robert. 1982. *Toward an Aesthetic of Reception*, translated by Timothy Bahti. Theory and History of Literature, vol. 2. Minneapolis: University of Minnesota Press.

Polanyi, Michael. 1958. *Personal Knowledge: Towards a Post-Critical Philosophy*. Chicago: University of Chicago Press.

Rosenblatt, Louise M. 1983. *Literature as Exploration*. 4th ed. New York: Modern Language Association.

Rosenblatt, Louise M. 1987. *The Reader, the Text, the Poem: The Transactional Theory of the Literary Work*. Carbondale, Ill.: Southern Illinois University Press.

Simpson, Louis. 1970. My Father in the Night Commanding No. In *Man in the Poetic Mode 6*. Evanston, Ill.: McDougal Littel.

2 Literature in the Secondary School: What Is and What Should Be

Ken Watson
University of Sydney
New South Wales, Australia

Ken Watson continues Probst's call for a response-centered curriculum in which reading is a creative process. His hope for literature instruction is the development of enthusiastic, autonomous, and committed readers. He believes this goal is more likely to be achieved when students become active collaborators with the text, confident of their own responses, rather than passive recipients of a teacher's narrowly directive instruction. Watson surveys both practical classroom ideas and a number of appealing British, American, and Australian novels that are consistent with and promote this collaboration.

Toronto Airport. Like most airports, ugly and impersonal. I have just flown in from Edmonton where I have been attending a conference of the Canadian Council of Teachers of English. With a four-hour wait before my flight to Amsterdam and London, I am about to settle down with a book when I realize that there may be a departure tax to pay. I walk up to the Canadian Pacific counter to inquire.

A man in his early thirties asks to look at my ticket. When he sees that I have a round-the-world ticket from Sydney, his face lights up. He tells me that he grew up in Sydney. I remark that, judging by his Canadian accent, he must have left Australia some time ago. He says that he left at the age of eighteen to avoid being conscripted for Vietnam. We talk briefly about that unhappy time; he tells me that his best friend, a part-Aboriginal boy, was conscripted and died in battle.

He asks what has brought me to Canada. When I tell him, he begins to talk about his school experiences. He tells me that his name is Joe and that he came to Australia from Italy at the age of eight. "I didn't like primary school—the kids called me 'wog' and I didn't know why—but I loved high school. I was bigger—could look after myself. I went to Ibrox Park High School; do you know it? I loved English. For the first three years we had Miss Woods—a great teacher. With her, reading stories and poems became a window on the world. Then we had the English master—I forget his name, but he was a good teacher, too. And the books we studied! Do you know *Huckleberry Finn*? And *The Crucible*? A great play. And poetry—

> My name is Ozymandias, king of kings:
> Look on my works, ye Mighty, and despair!

Great stuff! Do you know *Antony and Cleopatra*? You know, when I read the play at school I thought Cleopatra was a bitch, but I reread it a couple of years ago and I think she really loved him. Do you know John Donne? My favourite poet."

Suddenly he begins to recite. The words ring out across the empty airport lounge:

> Busie old foole, unruly Sunne,
> Why dost thou thus,
> Through windowes and through curtaines call on us?
> Must to thy motions lovers'
> seasons run?
> Saucy pedantique wretch, goe
> chide
> Late schoole boyes and sowre
> prentices,
> Goe tell Court-huntsmen, that
> the King will ride,
> Call countrey ants to harvest
> offices;
> Love, all alike, no season knowes,
> nor clime,
> Nor houres, dayes, months, which
> are the rags of time. . . .

When I finally board my plane, I find that my travelling companion is a man in his fifties, on a six-month world tour. I ask him which place he has liked best so far. He tells me that Manila has proved the best, because there the women were easy to find and very cheap. Fiji was disappointing, for the women were hard to find; in Vancouver, they were too expensive. He has, however, high hopes for Amsterdam. He asks me why I have been in Canada. When I tell him, he begins a tirade on the state of English teaching. There has, he tells me, been a steady decline since the 1950s. Since then, too much time has been spent on frills like literature and creative writing and too little time on grammar. As a result, the young cannot write; worse, they lack moral fibre. The ills of the world are laid at the English teacher's door.

I close my eyes, and think of Miss Woods, of the nameless English master, and of the words of John Donne echoing across an empty airport lounge. . . .

The example of Joe reminds us that English teachers can make a difference. Largely through the intervention of his teachers (though it is not impossible that his parents played a part in the process), Joe has become an enthusiastic and autonomous reader. For him there is no disjuncture between literature and other uses of language. One can guess at some lively teaching, relevant in the best sense of the word. But for every Joe that the schools produce, there is a Bill, a Harry, or a Susan for whom literature means, if it means anything at all, something quite remote from everyday experiences. Indeed, the teaching they have received seems to have had the reverse effect. A recent survey has revealed that while 26 percent of boys and 17 percent of girls in year (i.e., grade) 5 in Australian schools do not read any books outside of school, by year 11 the figures have risen to 51 percent for boys and 35 percent for girls (Bunbury et al., forthcoming).

It is not difficult to suggest reasons for the failure of the schools to produce able and committed readers of literature. In 1966, the delegates to the Dartmouth Seminar called for a "response-centered curriculum" (Squire 1971). Twenty years later, the words of John Dixon still apply: there is still a "widespread and self-defeating refusal. . . . to see that literature cannot be 'taught' by a direct approach, and that the teacher who weighs in with talk or lecture is more likely to kill a personal response than to support or develop it" (1969, 58).

The "cultural heritage" model that Dixon identified has developed into Ian Reid's (1984) "Gallery" model, which "isolates and immobilises." We are still failing to recognize the dangers of a premature demand for analysis, still failing to give due weight to the felt response. It is little wonder that so many of those who arrive at universities intending to study English still distrust their personal responses to literature, and those whose career choices lead them in other directions too often feel that they lack the capacity to enjoy or understand "works of literature."

A central problem may well be the lack of continuity in literary study. Jack Thomson (1987) suggests that there are stages of growth in literary response, and that any attempt to move students from the stage of "unreflective interest in action" to "reflecting on the signifi-

cance of events (theme) and behaviour (distanced evaluation of characters)" without giving them the opportunity to experience the
stages of "empathising" and "analogising" is likely to short-circuit
response.

For many years, some of us have been advocating a workshop approach to the teaching of English, but in practice this has too often
been confined to writing, with the reading of literature somehow set
apart. However, Ian Reid (1984) has presented a powerful argument
for a "Workshop" model of literary study which he contrasts with
the "Gallery" model mentioned earlier. Reid's model is "integrative
and interactive":

> Integration in the Workshop is of several kinds: of the world of
> play with the world of work: of literary utterances with ordinary
> uses of language: of verbal communication with other media of
> cultural expression: of reading with writing: and of cultural
> products with their means of production. (13)

In the Australian context, the advocacy of a professor of English
may prove to be just what is needed to convince the majority of
English teachers to adopt more productive ways of achieving their
goals.

Reading Literature: A Creative Process

Where do we go from here? The first essential would seem to be a
much wider acceptance of a model of reading literature that views it
as a *creative* process. Louise Rosenblatt, in her seminal *The Reader,
the Text, the Poem* (1978, 12) has argued powerfully that a poem (and
by this she means any work of literature) is "an event in time," the
result of a particular reader acting on a particular text. This is something that writers have long known. Walt Whitman wrote that the
reader "'must himself or herself construct indeed the poem, argument, history, metaphysical essay—the text furnishing the hints, the
clue, the start or frame-work" (quoted in Rosenblatt 1978, 175). And
W. H. Auden has written that "'what a poem means is the outcome
of a dialogue between the words on the page and the person who
happens to be reading it: that is to say, its meaning varies from person to person" (1973, 210).

Acceptance of this view of reading means that the reader's initial
responses must be given greater recognition than is often the case in
the classroom. Students need to feel that their initial questions and
associations as they read a text are worthwhile. Michael Benton and

Geoff Fox recommend that young readers be encouraged to keep reading logs in which "they respond in any way they choose to a novel, including speculations about how the story will develop, judgments, comparisons with their own experience, illustrations of characters, reflections on moments or themes from the book, comments on how the author is telling the story" (1985, 121).

Lola Brown, reflecting on her reading of Eleanor Spence's *A Candle for St. Antony*, notes that her "actual dialogue with the author has been at the level of remembering, speculating, associating," but that her teaching of such novels has been very different: "What I select to talk about in class is the product of *retrospective vision*, while students are still involved in the process of acquiring the author's world" (1982, 34). Like Benton and Fox, Brown concludes that it is important for the teacher to tap into, and value, what James Britton has described as "an unspoken monologue of responses—a fabric of comment, speculation, relevant autobiography" by some such means as a response journal.

A Wider Definition of Literature

Schools need to adopt a much wider definition of literature, one that will include not only novels, poems, and plays, but also nonfiction, film, and documentary; not only the works of recognized authors, but also the poems and stories of the pupils themselves; not only written works, but also the oral tradition. Ronald Blythe (1969) in Britain and Peter Moss (1977) in Australia have shown us that a vigorous tradition of oral narrative survives despite television and tabloids. Such material should be explored and created in the classroom-as-literary-workshop.

The Class Text: A Shared Experience

Some teachers, noting the failure of the schools to produce committed readers, have suggested that the villain is the class text. They argue that, in any class, tastes and abilities vary so much that the imposition of a single text is bound to be counterproductive. Yet there is evidence that the very sharing of reading experiences that can come when a common text is being studied can increase appreciation and understanding. Joe's enthusiasm for *Huckleberry Finn*, *The Crucible*, and the poems of John Donne is the product of such a shared experience. Lola Brown writes: "It strikes me that if our ability to make the world of a novel 'real' depends very much on the experiences we bring to it, sharing those experiences might trigger appropriate ones in other people or fill in the gaps where they have none to bring" (1982, 36). For the class text to work positively, it needs, as Lola Brown suggests, to be taught in the way that it is read. Instead of explicit teaching about the literary devices the author has used to construct the "reality" of the text, there needs to be a much more tentative approach on the teacher's part. The teacher must recognize that different readers will create different "poems" and that the refining of response is done far more effectively in the context of small-group discussion than in teacher-directed question-and-answer sessions. Certainly, teachers must abandon once and for all those teaching strategies, such as reading round the class and chapter-by-chapter summaries, that have been shown to be counterproductive.

Second, there needs to be a much more careful choice of texts for class study, especially if the class members differ in abilities. It is essential not only that the text have wide appeal, but also that it offer something for both the most and least able. Too many teachers seem unaware that they are living in what has been called the second golden age of children's literature (and the first golden age of adolescent literature!). There is, particularly as far as the novel is concerned, a wealth of British, North American, and Australian books from which to choose. Natalie Babbitt's *Tuck Everlasting*, Betsy Byars's *The Eighteenth Emergency* and *The Cartoonist*, Ivan Southall's *Let the Balloon Go*, Patricia Wrightson's *The Nargun and the Stars*, Rosemary Sutcliff's *Dragon Slayer*, Gene Kemp's *The Turbulent Term of Tike Tyler*, Jan Needle's *My Mate Shofiq*, Simon French's *Cannily, Cannily*, all appeal strongly to twelve and thirteen year olds. Further up the secondary school, the choice becomes a little harder, but there is still a wide range: Leon Garfield's *Smith* and *The Strange Affair of Adelaide Harris*, S. E. Hinton's *The Outsiders*, Ruth Park's *Playing Beatie Bow*, Robert O'Brien's *Z for Zachariah*, Felice Holman's *Slake's Limbo*, M. E. Kerr's *The Son of Someone Famous*, and Harper Lee's *To Kill a Mockingbird* are all possibilities. If some members of the class are such poor readers that the teacher has to read much of the book aloud, this hardly matters; there is increasing evidence that pupils of all ages benefit from frequently hearing good reading of prose as well as of poetry.

"Instant Book," a teaching idea described in Robert Protherough's *Developing Response to Fiction* (1983), is particularly useful in giving pupils in mixed-ability classes a sense of the novel as a whole. At the end of a unit on the novel, the teacher (or a group of pupils) makes a selection of twenty or so passages which, when read in sequence (perhaps with a few links from a narrator) give an overview of the story. Each pupil is given a passage to prepare overnight; a dramatic reading is then presented with the class seated in a circle. The method has the added advantage of provoking vigorous discussion concerning whether the most important sections of the book have been included; it is also being used as an effective means of review in senior classes preparing for public examinations.

How many such texts should be studied by the class as a whole? A sampling of some twelve or so good English departments in Sydney schools suggests that the favoured number is two per term (in a three-term year). At least up to year 10, these books are frequently studied in units that involve pupils in those active explorations of text which Stratta, Dixon, and Wilkinson (1973) have called "imaginative re-creation." The class study of Leon Garfield's _Smith_, for example, might involve pupils in preparing a newspaper report of the death of Mr. Field, designing "wanted" posters for Smith and Lord Tom, writing and recording on cassette a radio adaptation of the most exciting sections of the story, and compiling a glossary of the eighteenth-century terms used in the novel. They might also read Alfred Noyes's poems _The Ballad of Dick Turpin_ and _The Highwayman_ (the latter in the edition superbly illustrated by Charles Keeping), and dip into Garfield's _Apprentices_ series, which provides memorable pictures of aspects of eighteenth-century life. After reading Hans Peter Richter's _The Time of the Young Soldiers_, a class might, in groups, sift through photographs of Nazi Germany and the Second World War, with the object of selecting those which best illustrate the novel, and read a selection of war poems in order to choose one that could appropriately be placed at the beginning of the book.

Among the other techniques that can be employed to encourage active response are improvisation and the preparation of sections of the text for semi-dramatic presentation. The various books on reader's theatre and the recent publication _Exploring Texts through Reading Aloud and Dramatization_ by Anne Newbould and Andrew Stibbs (1983) provide many suggestions.

Wide-Reading Scheme

It is increasingly being recognized that a wide-reading scheme should go hand in hand with the class study of selected texts. Many teachers set aside one period a week for wide reading (by teacher as well as by pupils), drawing on a class library or book box as well as on the school library. Others have persuaded the English department, or even the whole school, to set aside time each day for USSR (Uninterrupted Sustained Silent Reading) or DEAR (Drop Everything and Read); the value of such activity is being increasingly supported by research. (For example, Trelease 1984 cites some American studies of younger readers, and Kefford 1982, in a two-year study, found clear evidence of improvement in reading ability.) Swinburne Technical School in Melbourne has gone a step further in encouraging reading at home through its program RIB-IT (Read in Bed—It's Terrific) (Goodman 1982).

One point that ought to be made about the wide-reading scheme is that it is not essential that there be follow-up activity after each book read. The requirement that a book report or review be written after each book has been completed seems likely to make reluctant readers even more unwilling to read. Another point to be borne in mind is that the wide-reading scheme (and, indeed, the texts chosen for class study) should include some nonfiction—which is preferred by a sizable minority of readers. Annette Smith (1982), surveying the reading of pupils in years 9 and 10 in five secondary schools, found that many of the students chose nonfiction in preference to fiction. These students cited such books as the animal stories of James Herriot and Gerald Durrell, stories of the Second World War, such as Paul Brickhill's *Reach for the Sky* and Esther Hautzig's autobiographical *The Endless Steppe*, and books dealing with special interests, such as ballet.

Conclusion

Teaching that is informed by the notion of the reader as active collaborator with the author in the making of meaning, that values and builds upon initial responses and does not strive to impose a particular viewpoint is much more likely to succeed than the narrowly directive teaching one can still find in some of our secondary schools. Workshop treatments of literature, as advocated in Stratta, Dixon, and Wilkinson's *Patterns of Language* (1973) and more recently in Ian Reid's *The Making of Literature* (1984), combined with classroom encouragement of wide reading, will lead to involvement, heightened enjoyment, and ultimately to reflection and more fully formulated responses. Further, such approaches will give students that power over discourse that is essential if they are to become fully autonomous readers and writers.

References

Auden, W. H. 1973. How Can I Tell What I Think till I See What I Say? In *New Movements in the Study and Teaching of English*, edited by N. Bagnall. London: Temple Smith.

Benton, Michael, and Geoff Fox. 1985. *Teaching Literature: Nine to Fourteen*. Oxford: Oxford University Press.

Blythe, Ronald. 1969. *Akenfield*. Harmondsworth, England: Penguin.

Brown, Lola. 1982. Do We Teach the Way We Read? *English in Australia* 62 (October): 33–36. Also in *English Teaching: An International Exchange*, edited by James Britton. London: Heinemann Educational, 1984.

Bunbury, Rhonda, et al. Forthcoming. *Children's Choice*.

Dixon, John. 1969. *Growth through English*. 2d ed. Oxford Studies in Education. Oxford: Oxford University Press.

Goodman, Jo. 1982. *RIB-IT*. Melbourne, Australia: Victorian Association for the Teaching of English.

Kefford, Rod. 1982. Sustained Silent Reading: Does It Work? *Developments in English Teaching* 1 (2): 23–27.

Moss, Peter. 1977. *Telling Tales*. Melbourne: Australian International Press/ Curriculum Development Centre.

Newbould, Anne, and Andrew Stibbs. 1983. *Exploring Texts through Reading Aloud and Dramatization*. London: Ward Lock.

Protherough, Robert. 1983. *Developing Response to Fiction*. Milton Keynes, England: Open University Press.

Reid, Ian. 1984. *The Making of Literature*. Adelaide, Australia: Australian Association for the Teaching of English.

Rosenblatt, Louise. 1978. *The Reader, the Text, the Poem: The Transactional Theory of the Literary Work*. Carbondale: Southern Illinois University Press.

Smith, Annette. 1982. Non-Fiction in the English Class. *Developments in English Teaching* 1 (2): 33–36.

Squire, James. 1971. Toward a Response-Oriented Curriculum in Literature. In *New English, New Imperatives*, edited by H. B. Maloney. Urbana, Ill.: National Council of Teachers of English.

Stratta, Leslie, John Dixon, and Andrew Wilkinson. 1973. *Patterns of Language*. London: Heinemann Educational.

Thomson, Jack. 1987. *Understanding Teenagers' Reading: Reading Processes and the Teaching of Literature*. New York: Nichols.

Trelease, Jim. 1984. *The Read-Aloud Handbook*. Harmondsworth, England: Penguin.

3 Developing Responses to Character in Literature

John Dixon
London, England

Leslie Stratta
Defford, Worcestershire, England

John Dixon and Leslie Stratta ask two fundamentally simple and important questions: What happens when we read or watch fiction? Do the formal exercises of our schooling deny or advance this elementary event? They believe, with Probst and Watson, that readers should be more than passive mechanisms on which texts make unproblematic, definitive imprints, the same for everyone. Particularly, the traditional character questions posed in classrooms, in assignments in standard textbooks, and on examinations betray "false assumptions about the act of reading, the kind of knowledge to be derived from literature, and the kinds of writing that help to articulate it." Dixon and Stratta use actual student writing as evidence of this ingrained tradition and of creative and specific alternatives to it. Their aim is to encourage students' imaginative penetration and insight, to invite them to participate in the complex process of constructing characters in their imaginations.

Why do we read fiction, watch television dramas, and go to plays? Among the reasons, there is often the feeling that we may have something to learn—however indirectly—about ourselves and other human beings. We put ourselves in the characters' places, we interpret what's happening to them as a commentary on what's actually happening to us, and we suffer or enjoy the consequences. Or, at times, we stand back and look at what's happening to them—feeling pained, grimly amused, or delighted for their sakes—and we say to ourselves, "Yes, that's what people are really like." Equally, at other times, we say to the writer or director, "How untrue! What a mean view of people you have. How little you understand social life."

25

This is a modest enough view, we would say, of the things we and teachers like ourselves actually do while reading or watching poetic fiction, but we offer it quite deliberately here. The reason is simple: these elementary events are often denied in the formative exercises that generations of students have been put through at school or college. (And some of the new "critical theory" denies them, too.) To be specific, these exercises assume that you do not create a character in your imagination as you read, that you do not feel sympathy or antipathy to those personae on the screen, that you never test their reality against life as you know it, that you can't read the play as a metaphor for parts of your own life, and that you won't challenge the author's conception of people and society.

Only very powerful institutions can deny such obvious facts. In the case of the United Kingdom, the preuniversity exams have provided the appropriate institution; elsewhere, the assignments in standard textbooks have done the job. But both derive from commonplace practices in universities. We have to begin, then, by challenging the rationality of such practices.

An Engrained Tradition

Let us start with the assignments or "questions" as they are called in the United Kingdom. How often have we been asked (or asked our students) to describe *the* character of some personage in a drama? Or to describe *the* changes in her character? Or to point to *the* ways in which X and Y are different? Let us stop for a moment and inspect these commonplace wordings. What tacit assumptions do they carry? They suggest that, somehow or other, definitive answers are possible. It is not how you imagine a character that counts; instead it is your ability to describe something already existing and defined. Other words enforce a similar message: what "*is revealed* to us" in scene two, "*what impressions are created* by" this chapter, "what *do we* [all] *learn*," and "what is *the effect* on *the* reader." Such wordings assume that a reader is a passive mechanism to which texts do things and that all readers by rights should think the same. It seems that what the examiner (in this case) wants to hear about is not your reading of a play, but your (more or less adequate) version of what "the reader" ought to be thinking and feeling.[1]

Not surprisingly, when they are talked about in this way, characters often seem to be objects. The constructive processes of the imagination can be eliminated.

What do such tasks do to students? They give students the messages that "the character" is something that must be talked about in an impersonal way and in summary terms. Characters become bundles of traits, of "points you make" in "your answer" to a question. Students "refer to the text" only to "illustrate" these general points, and they try to make them sound definitive and consensual, as requested.

Under these constraints, most students tend to write, understandably, like linguistic cripples. They lose contact with their actual experience as readers because it seems to be ruled out of court. This is demonstrable, too: Recently one of us codirected an investigation of writing produced by the elite student population in the United Kingdom, those in the specialist, preuniversity literature course (Dixon and Brown 1984–85). A sample of the writings was read by a distinguished panel of teachers from schools, colleges, and universities. The panel (which included the other author) found that well over half the sample showed either "rather thin" or "very thin, weak or negative" evidence of "a genuine encounter with the book, play or poem."

To see what this implies, let us look at a representative student from the higher grades, someone fairly certain of a place in an honours degree course in literature. This seventeen or eighteen year old has been asked to write about Shakespeare's Cleopatra, and, being in a specialist course, has graduated from "describing the character," which is the norm at this age. Now the student is faced with an invented quotation (about Cleopatra's "infinite variety" but lack of "complexity") and given the standard instruction to "discuss." What happens in the opening paragraphs?

> Schucking commented that the Cleopatra of the first Act "would not make any self sacrifice for anybody," and yet at the end of the play she commits suicide to join Antony. This change throughout the play from the selfish Egyptian Cleopatra to the almost-Roman Cleopatra at her death does add complexity to her character which is otherwise fairly clear cut.
>
> That she is "infinitely varied" is clear in the first Act. She constantly taunts Antony and when he has seen a messenger from Rome she asks a servant to go to Antony. If Antony is sad the servant should report that "I am dancing. If in mirth say I am sudden sick." She constantly sets herself at odds with his mood because this, she knows, is part of her enchantment. She is beautiful to the extent that a Roman soldier known for his common-sense declares that "She beggars all description." The impression that she is almost magical is conveyed in the descriptions of her by others. She is called an "enchanting queen" and

a "serpent of old Nile" by Antony. As Mrs. Jameson com-
mented, she is a mixture between "Eastern voluptuousness and
gypsy's magic." The whole atmosphere that she and Egypt per-
vade is sensual. Antony describes "The beds in the East" as
"soft" and Enobarbus says "He will to his Egyptian dish again."
However part of her charm lies in the double nature of her character: she is quite capable of being just as cruel, scheming and
harsh as she is of being voluptuous. Her cruelty is shown, for
example, by the effect that the messenger carrying news of Antony's marriage to Octavia has on her. She says: "I'll spurn
thine eyes like balls before me and unhair thy head." We learn
at the end of the play that she has carried out numerous experiments to find the least painful way to die, presumably on her
servants or prisoners. She has a shrewd political sense, she realizes after Caesar has declared that he cannot be "ungentle" that
"he words me." She is also extremely jealous of "the married
woman" throughout the play.

The student has been instructed to write about Cleopatra in terms
of two highly general traits, her "infinite variety," but lack of "complexity." How does one deal with this? This student starts by taking
each in turn, opening with "complexity." Looking at the whole
play, he or she posits a change from "the selfish Egyptian Cleopatra
to the almost-Roman." The student takes no credit for this "reading"; instead it is attributed—slightly ambiguously—to an au-
thoritative critic. On that evidence, complexity can be affirmed,
though "her character . . . is otherwise fairly clear-cut." (Does the
student feel perhaps that she or he ought to be able to assign a definitive character to Cleopatra, according to the rules of the game?)

The second paragraph turns to "infinite variety." How is this to
be dealt with, in appropriately general terms? The student tries a list
of traits:

—she constantly sets herself at odds with [Antony's] mood

—she is beautiful

—she is almost magical [fortified by another quoted authority]

—she is voluptuous . . . sensual

—[but] she is cruel, scheming and harsh

—she has a shrewd political sense

—she is also extremely jealous

Phrases quoted from various parts of the play support these points.

The student is understandably caught. A "change" such as
Schucking (or the student) posits could only be traced by close attention to certain key scenes. But the examiner's demand is for a

summary discussion of Cleopatra throughout the play, in terms of an arbitrary (and confused) opposition: "not complex, but infinitely varied." How will the second half of the essay deal with this?

> I think that she convinces us and Antony of her love for him and her descriptions of him certainly convey this. She seems almost to sublimate him, she calls him "The demi-Atlas of the world" and compares him to "Mars" constantly using world imagery to show his force. Yet despite this love she refuses to descend from the Monument in case she is seized by Caesar's men and Antony must be lifted to her despite his condition.
>
> Some of her observations reveal her acuteness. For example when Antony is marveling at the speed of Caesar she says aptly: "Celerity is never more admired than by the negligent." and in this act we see Cleopatra constantly building up to suicide to join her love of men. Her final speech is comparable to Antony's death and seems more Roman in tone for it is more restrained than we might perhaps have expected from her earlier outbursts. She has no tears in this last scene and she is longing to die so that she may greet "her husband." We do not know whether in the previous Act she did betray Antony to Caesar, as Antony accused her but it seems improbable because of her great love for him.
>
> As A. C. Bradley commented "everything about her intoxicated Antony's senses: her wiles and her taunts, her furies and meltings, her laughter and tears—all bewitched him alike." All these characteristics are shown to be part of her "infinite variety" however the complexity in her character can be seen by the fact that she loved Antony and yet was too selfish to come down from the monument. This suggests still the attitude that claims that she is totally selfish, yet in contrast to this she cannot live without Antony so she cannot have realised this at the monument or she would surely have descended to join him. Many critics have tried to decipher this problem and it seems to them that perhaps she did not realize the extent of her love until after Antony's death, and this does seem to be the only possible conclusion.
>
> Her character certainly has "infinite variety" but I would disagree that she "is not in the least complex" because of this almost Roman suicide in Act V. Also part of her "infinite variety" is the fact that she is difficult to fathom and unpredictable and thus again this, in itself, suggests a complexity of character.

Interestingly, the second half opens with a change of voice: "*I think* that she convinces us and Antony." However, the moment fades: "*We see* Cleopatra constantly building up to suicide"; A. C. Bradley's characteristics "*are shown to be* part of her"; and—where even critics are unsure—one has to report on behalf of the majority what seems "to be the only possible solution." Then, in the final sentence, comes a hint of a personal note: "she is difficult to fathom"! It would be an unusually wise seventeen or eighteen year old who could feel otherwise, we would suggest, but traditional assignments have no room for doubts, puzzlement, mixed feelings, surprise, or baffled uncertainties. If you still feel that way about Cleopatra, so much the worse for you!

We have every sympathy for such students. They are asked to argue with a proposition, not to explore a complex character. It is assumed that the whole text must be covered; thus, the critical scene in Act V cannot be dwelt on with detailed attention. There is nothing in the tradition to encourage personal readings and interpretations, everything to suggest the superior authority of (an assumed) critical consensus, deciphering the problems.

Of course, someone steeped in the tradition might still see "a student who has enjoyed and grasped a good deal of the contradiction s/he observes in Cleopatra. Most of the quotations are well used, genuinely integrated with comment." This was actually said by an experienced examiner. A more deserved comment, in our view, places this as "in many ways a typical exam piece; the focus is on the question, the literature is there mainly to illustrate the points made. This writer comes nearest to the play when s/he sees it in terms of a 'problem'. . . . But the given topic doesn't seem to help her/him get close to Cleopatra" (Dixon and Brown 1984–85).

We have analysed here in some detail what happens to an able student in an elite literature course. What happens to the majority has to be left to your imagination. Evidently they will struggle much less successfully in the clutches of the question (and the critics). Yet, in our view, it is not so much the students as the traditional demands that deserve serious criticism. For such questions make demonstrably false assumptions about the act of reading, the kind of knowledge to be derived from literature, and the kinds of writing that help to articulate it.

What's more, they treat literature as if it existed ineffably somewhere in outer space, not here in real societies. Cleopatra, with her "shrewd political sense," is actually placed in a world dominated by the triumvirs, the three men at the top in the Roman empire. As you or I direct the play (in imagination or for real) how do we "read" her role vis à vis the men's? What perspective on these imperial triumvirs do we set up? (And, as we do so, what do we discover about the author's apparent position?)

Today, gender and imperial power are recognised as crucial elements in historical experience. How can we "direct" the play without considering its implications for these human issues? Isn't it essential to consider the tacit and explicit ideology of our "reading" (and to make discoveries as we do so about the author's positions on women and history)?

An Alternative Strategy

Learning to "read" literature (including learning to act or direct a scene) involves a complex process of constructing characters and their world in your imagination. It is very easy to do so crudely. Indeed we are bombarded with stereotyped characters every day. Think of the news bulletins (or the advertising) we watch on television. How many people in them appear simply as beautiful and voluptuous? or shrewd and scheming? or harsh or cruel? The general traits attributed to Cleopatra are familiar enough; all that has altered is the mixture. Indeed it is difficult to expect a lot more if the demand is for characters to be reduced to traits.

Literature itself offers a different kind of possibility. Starting from the text, we can construct people in action, people responding to each other, people living their lives moment by moment. The novel—and at times, drama—can also give privileged access to their thoughts and feelings on such occasions. This is the characteristic kind of "knowledge" that the text suggests we construct. It is quite different, of course, from the unproblematic, definitive knowledge assumed by traditional "character" questions.

What is an appropriate language to use with students about such a process? There have been valuable experiments conducted recently in the United Kingdom when a group of teachers persuaded the Cambridge examination board to let them try an alternative approach (Dixon and Brown 1984–85). These teachers started with the following assumptions:

1. It is folly to ask students to write without having the text available (something we would never think of doing ourselves).
2. Given a long text, there needs to be a focus on a selected chapter or scene.
3. When students are re-exploring and imaginatively reconstructing an already familiar scene, writing gets a valuable springboard.
4. It is natural to refer out from that scene to contrasts, developments, and parallels elsewhere in the text.

Thus the nature of the questions changes. "What are your reactions as you read through?" they ask. "Are there any lines that particularly interest or puzzle you?" "Your feelings may vary," of course, as the scene unfolds, but "when you look closely at what each of the characters says and you think about how he or she says it, what impression do you form?" "Do you find anything unexpected in their behaviour (or attitude or language)?" "Any differences in temperament and the way they look at life?"[2]

Language such as this elicits a very different understanding of Cleopatra. It also leaves room for us to ask how she is affected by Antony's presence and by his absence. Ambivalent feelings are allowed. Lines may still be puzzling and may express conflicting, ambiguous intentions.

There is room, if the text offers a foundation, for characters to be complex and for subtle changes to occur over time. Students are being encouraged to reread or to act out a scene again, to become involved in it and to search as they do so for the more delicate cues about what is going on between people. The aim is to affect their imaginative penetration and insight into what might be constructed—how to realise characters in action.

What does the act of writing do, then, at this point? It opens the way for insight that might otherwise be tacit (or half implicit) to become more fully articulated. Of course, students may well have discussed the scene in groups, before and after acting it perhaps, but after that experience, writing gives the individual time to crystallise from a personal standpoint what is being learned in the group.

So far we have been talking as if the characters are primarily unique people in a social group. They often are (though not in all fictions). However, there is a further possibility: that characters can be read as representative, too, so that the fictional work becomes a metaphor for life. Cleopatra is a general among generals; is the fact that she is a woman not significant? The contrast between Rome and Egypt suggests another form of representation in which she is an element (though it is often forgotton by examiners that the contrast is between new imperial centre and ancient, but dominated, satellite). *Antony and Cleopatra*, following on *Julius Caesar*, suggests that wider historical processes may be represented. And so on.

Reading off these and similar metaphors from the fictional work calls for a further use of imaginative intelligence. It is an independent creative activity. Even when the characters are manifestly types, as with the pigs, the cart horse, and the sheep in *Animal Farm*, what they represent to readers manifestly changes over the decades—and is inevitably affected by a reader's own ideological stance. Where characters appear unique, or there is only the merest hint they might also be types, imagining what they might signify is a complex act. Yet we all do it.

Most of the U.K. exam questions that we are currently surveying seem to ignore this process altogether. At first this seems surprising; after all, the tradition is to invite generalized statements about the character—to treat each as a type with a definitive set of traits—and to neglect the interplay between characters. Perhaps the reason is a hidden assumption that people in general are not socially and culturally shaped by the ethnic group, social class, and society they live in, and thus don't ever behave in representative ways?

Whatever the reason, it does seem to us important to register the fact that students, like us, find some behaviour typical, representative, even symbolic. But to avoid overstereotyping, it seems essential to begin from the particular, as the Cambridge group are doing (Dixon and Brown 1984–85). Having done that first, it then makes better sense to ask about the typical, too, to think about characters like Sir Walter Elliot and Mr. Collins, or Sir Leicester Dedlock and Mr. Rouncewell, or even Piggy and Ralph, and what they stand for.

The Cambridge group have made just one or two efforts in this direction. For instance, after asking students to read chapter 3 of *Lord of the Flies*, they say: "Golding tells us how Ralph and Jack walked along, 'two continents of experience and feeling, unable to communicate.' . . . Explore the differences between these 'two continents.'" The metaphor of the two "continents" (an interesting choice!) points to a typification the author is aware of. As an unseen exam question, this seems far too difficult for the average U.K. student, especially in the absence of an adequate tradition to support it. However, the idea of exploring such possibilities, first in classroom discussion, then in writing, does seem a necessary extension of the alternative approach to character. Beyond that, we must be tentative for the moment for lack of detailed evidence. And we should be interested to hear from any other groups who have begun to take seriously this view of character as type.

Investigating the Alternatives

This is a stage in our knowledge of English teaching when widespread classroom investigations are needed to discover new possibilities for character studies by students aged fourteen to eighteen.

Before offering some general guidelines, let us look at one such investigation carried out by Jean Blunt, a high school English teacher. After a discussion with us about the limitations of the traditional approach, she asked a group of her fifteen to sixteen year olds who were working on *Billy Liar* to choose a section that they felt was important for the central relationship—that between Billy and Liz. "What do you notice about Billy's behaviour and attitude?" she asked them. "What explanations would you offer for it, bearing in mind what you know about him up to this point?" Think "what significance, if any, this scene has for what happens to Billy later in the novel."

Such language invites a personal reading, with a movement from perceptions to explanations and then—if the student felt it—to any wider significance of the action. Let us see how one of the group, Anthony, responded. We begin with the opening half of his study of chapter 8.

As Billy enters the shop with Arthur he does so almost rowdily. He wants to ridicule Maurie, the owner. "We opened the door with our feet and almost fell into the shop." Billy wants to be noticed and puts on a false front of bravado. The crowd of youths in the X-L Disc Bar make Billy feel old-fashioned and unfashionable. He is conscious of his scruffy appearance. He tries to put on an "intellectual act." Arthur leaves Billy and is lost in the crowded sea of people. Billy feels isolated and lonely and knows nobody. He is almost glad to hear Stamp's voice. Stamp sees him and tells of Shadrock adding up Billy's postage book. Billy feels ill because of his business with the calendars' postage money. He is ridiculed a little by Stamp's crowd of hangers on. He gets annoyed at Stamp and is in a confused state, uncertain of what to do when Stamp tells him: "Your mate's upstairs."

He knows Stamp means Liz. He immediately feels calmer, past memories of her come flooding into his brain, cleansing it of other thoughts. ". . . all thoughts of Shadrock going out of my head before it took out." His mind is a kaleidoscope of thoughts, memories, rehearsed snippets of things he will say to her. She is a port for him to shelter in, in his present stormy situation. "I walked slowly up the stairs, the noise fading into a cacophonous backwash."

He sees Liz, serving a customer, he puts off the moment of meeting. Billy tries to settle down. ("I was trying on expressions as though I carried a mirror about with me.") He can find no sensation or emotion of her.

When they finally speak, Billy does so very honestly without false bravado or reversion to Ambrosia. Liz brings out the best in him and he feels calm and secure in her presence. He likes her mystery, her enigma and he likes the way she understands him, knows him. ("She was the only girl who knew how to grin.") As he leaves her presence, he feels he must do something to impress Stamp, so he reverts to what he came in for, puts on a false face and "takes the piss out of Maurie."

Anthony, as we see, begins with a narrative, a form that has been traditionally regarded for some reason as juvenile (as if the novel itself was a juvenile form of knowledge compared to the generalisations of critics!). Let us put aside this odd prejudice and ask instead what he is using narrative to do. In part, certainly, he is retelling the events. But interwoven with the string of events (as in all complex narrative) there is a strand of "commentary"—explanations, comments, interpretations:

—almost rowdily

—wants to ridicule/to be noticed

—puts on a false front of bravado

—feel[s] old-fashioned and unfashionable

—tries to put on an "intellectual act"

—almost glad to hear Stamp's voice

—in a confused state, uncertain of what to do

These interpretations of Billy in action go beyond the text but are in sympathy with the author. They "read" Billy's behaviour with delicacy and, taken together, form quite a complex analysis of his immediate state. When that changes, so does Anthony's language:

—memories . . . come flooding into his brain, cleansing it of other thoughts

—his mind is a kaleidoscope

—she is a port for him to shelter in

—tries to settle down

—can find no sensation or emotion of her

The importance of the inner events at this point is suggested by Anthony's metaphors. They testify to and express the impact of Liz and the knowledge that she is there. They also indicate a very understanding and involved reader of the text, we would add. There is a "genuine encounter" going on here already. The writing continues:

Billy needs Liz. She is the only one who understands Billy properly. She calms him down, makes him tell the truth. He realizes

she can do this. Billy never tries to spar off in his meetings with
Liz; he doesn't need to impress her, she respects him enough already. He understands Liz and she understands. Billy respects
her because she can leave town whenever she wants and he
cannot. He likes her "Bohemism" and "escapism." Billy likes
her and this is proved by his including of her in his Ambrosian
dreams.

I would expect Billy to react this way because of his previous
experiences with people, as at the Kit-Kat where he and Arthur
are joked about, but nobody greets them friendly.

Considering the book as a whole, the scene is very important
to us because it gives an in-depth view of Billy's character. We
see that, even with his own peer-group where he thinks he is
accepted as "one of the crowd," in his heart of hearts he knows
he is an outsider. He knows nobody and is friendly with nobody in the X-L Disc Bar. He often imagines that he does, but he
doesn't and this leads to uncertainty and insecurity.

"I stood by myself, hesitating. The odd thing was that he
seemed to know everybody and I didn't. In the No. 1 thinking it
was sometimes the other way round."

We also see more of his relationship with Liz. Even though
she does relax him he does not feel fully relaxed with her. He
still talked to her in cliches occasionally and does fool around
(such as pretending to have flat feet and walking accordingly
after coming out of the Roxy). But she can cure him of this by
saying, "Count to five and tell the truth." He realises this and
respects her power over him.

However at the very end of the novel, he still cannot make a
decision. Liz leaves without him and he cannot break his ties
with Stadhoughton, but he has come the closest he has ever
been to making a major decision in his life.

When generalisation does emerge from narrative, as here and frequently in novels, it has an active function: this student is generalis-
ing from immediately present and concrete perceptions. Thus the
rhythm of his paragraph starting "Billy needs Liz" has the force of a
discovery. But this paragraph is not enough for Anthony; he wants
to set the need for understanding and respect in its context, and, finally, to recognise that the relationship is not symmetrical. For all
Liz's benign "power," Billy is still unable to make a (crucial) decision, though the last concession ("the closest he has ever been")
suggests a positive significance to the experience.[3]

You would probably agree that the text of *Billy Liar* doesn't invite
the same complexity of imaginative construction as *Antony and
Cleopatra*. But this initial experiment of Jean Blunt's already exposes,
in our view, the fallacy of looking first at the text and only secondly,
if at all, at the room left by the assignment for students to articulate

their responses. So far as this evidence is concerned, we would have little difficulty in saying which student has got more out of the occasion—the seventeen- to eighteen-year-old specialist or the fifteen to sixteen year old. It is qualitative judgments of this kind that must steer further investigation in class and in examinations.

Suggested Guidelines for Further Investigation

1. Does the language of the assignment (or negotiated topic) indicate that the student is constructing a personal, imaginative experience, based on the printed text? Does it encourage students as they write to continue such imaginative work?

2. Does the topic or assignment allow the student to trace character(s) in action, to imagine people in relation to each other moment by moment? Is room left for narrative that comments and interprets from an imaginatively involved point of view?

3. Is there also an invitation to stand back and relate what happens in a specific scene (possibly chosen by students) to the way they now see that character in the action as a whole? Is there encouragement to keep any generalisations that emerge close to particularly telling moments in the action?

4. Is there a further recognition that characters may be viewed as types (within a constructed social microcosm) as well as unique individuals? Is there room for an intelligent discussion of character as type? If so, are students aware enough of particulars to avoid overstereotyping and stock response?

5. Are there any opportunities for students who are at odds with the author and the way a character has been conceived?

6. Are the forms of writing flexible enough to encapsulate any and all of these purposes, if necessary?

7. Will the students have real readers as well as you, the teacher? Will they get back interested, appreciative comments and positive criticism from their peers?

Notes

1. These wordings are taken from a selection of GCE O level questions set in 1985; for a more detailed analysis, see Dixon and Stratta (1985).

2. We are grateful to Jane Ogborn for bringing these questions to our attention; for further analysis, see Dixon and Stratta (1985).

3. We are grateful to Jean Blunt and Anthony Price of Summerhill School, Kingswinford, Dudley, for making this work available and for their cooperation in this experiment.

References

Dixon, John, and John Brown. 1984–85. *Responses to Literature—What Is Being Assessed?* 2 vols. Schools Council. (Available from the National Association of Teachers of English, Birley School Annexe, Fox Lane, Frecheville, Sheffield S12 4WY, England.)

Dixon, John, and Leslie Stratta. 1985. *Character Studies—Changing the Question.* Southampton, England: Southern Regional Examination Board. (Available from the ERIC Document Reproduction Service, 3900 Wheeler Ave., Alexandria, VA 22304. ED 268 522.)

4 A Test-Driven Literary Response Curriculum

Patrick X. Dias
McGill University
Montreal, Quebec, Canada

The first three essays in this collection manifest the efforts to establish student-response-centered English instruction in the United States (Probst), Australia (Watson), and England (Dixon and Stratta). Patrick Dias goes on to explore the development of a student-centered literary response curriculum in Quebec, Canada, and the attempt to reconcile it with government-mandated school-leaving examinations. Knowing that tests define what is valued and dictate what is taught, he explores what we should evaluate in a response-to-literature program, what conditions we should establish that will allow students to respond fully and truly to literary texts. He then outlines his specific proposals for the sequence and tasks of an English composition and literature examination.

The words *test-driven* in this chapter's title suggest that the curriculum I am writing about has been tried and tested in the process of its being "sold." They also suggest that the curriculum is one that is supported rather than subverted by government-mandated tests and examinations. I intend *test-driven* in both these senses.

Curriculum Development in Quebec

In Quebec, as in most provinces of Canada, curriculum is centrally mandated by a ministry of education. The Quebec secondary language arts curriculum (hereafter referred to as the program) has come about through an extensive consultation with language arts consultants, teachers of English, and representatives of school boards, universities, parent-teacher groups, and teacher organizations (Ministère de l'Education 1982). These various interests have been represented on a committee that has overseen the production of curriculum documents written by several teams composed of members active in the field of English. In the process of developing these documents, team members have presented their proposals at annual conferences of teachers of English and invited teachers to try out the practices described and report back on their effectiveness. Thus the various documents that compose the program have gone through several revisions as teachers have fed back the results of trial runs.

This process has resulted in the 1982 publication of the official mandated program and its over twenty supporting documents that suggest how the program objectives can be implemented in the classroom. I offer this brief and simplified history of program development only to suggest the process of consultation involved; the program has, indeed, been test-driven. The new program is essentially the set of beliefs, understandings, and practices that are current among those English teachers in the province who have in one way or another participated in the development of the program. Officially, however, and for the larger number of English teachers in the province, the program is a set of objectives—global, general, and specific—that are in keeping with the format of the programs in other subject areas. The program also satisfies those curriculum experts at the centre who, generally speaking, are concerned that the program include a hierarchy of objectives specified as a set of student behaviours. Fortunately, the objectives are set within a context of explanations that draw on the likes of Vygotsky, Britton, Halliday, Dixon, Moffett, and Rosenblatt and that sufficiently discount any behaviouristic orientations that the format and some of the terminology evoke. Even more fortunately, those charged with writing the final version of the program resisted the demand to specify sets of objectives for each grade level, properly insisting that development in the language arts could and should not be specified along a continuum of sequentially graded objectives.

A Process-Oriented Curriculum

Despite its seemingly behaviouristic orientation, the program's underlying emphasis is on supporting the processes by which—and creating the contexts within which—adolescents can develop as language users, as speakers, writers, readers, and listeners. Thus the program places a high priority on collaborative activity: on group work that provides the need to use language in new and challenging ways; on feedback from peers and on group revision and editing of one's writing; on talking together to come to an understanding of a literary text. There is no indication in the program that a body of knowledge must be acquired, that certain literary terms are to be manipulated or grammatical concepts mastered. We have developed a program without "content," without set texts; a program that emphasizes process, language in use, and students' responses to literary texts; a program that assigns responsibility to the student for making meaning in reading and in writing. Such a program devalues the teacher's role as dispenser of knowledge, manager of content, and arbiter of correctness and the right meaning and, therefore, it presents formidable problems to teachers of English who are expected to prepare their students for provincewide and centrally set secondary school-leaving examinations.

Examinations and a Process-Oriented Curriculum

School-leaving examinations may seem antithetical to a process-based, student-centered program. And, as traditionally conceived, such examinations are inconsistent with the objectives of the program. In Quebec, at least, such examinations conjure up images of rows of desks in large gymnasiums, with invigilators, one eye on the clock, ready to hand out a stack of printed examinations and a set of injunctions. The new program is being implemented by grade level; it began in the first year of high school in 1983, and it will become compulsory for all grade levels by the end of 1988. However, since several schools have decided to adopt the new program *en bloc*, the Ministry of Education was forced to recognize that consideration of a new format for examinations could not be postponed until 1988.

The problem was not entirely unforeseen, and a beginning had been made in 1984 by providing in the English composition school-leaving examination an optional procedure: students, after having written their first, exploratory drafts, would be allowed to discuss these drafts with one or more members of their "writing groups" and thus would receive feedback. Such a procedure would not be foreign to those accustomed to sharing first drafts. The feedback session would take approximately twenty minutes, after which students would return to their desks to revise, edit, and rewrite.

By all accounts the optional procedure has been an unqualified success: students who had received peer feedback and were interviewed after the examination reported that they felt much more relaxed and therefore better able to compose themselves and their thoughts, that they were pleased with what they had written. Teachers who evaluated the writing report felt that, on the whole, students who used the optional procedure wrote much better than those who did not. Such results are not entirely unexpected; what is heartening is that many teachers who did not use the optional procedure concluded their students were at a disadvantage and are resolved to introduce group work into their writing classes. It is in this sense that we can speak of a test *driving* the curriculum. Even though the curriculum mandates such practice, it is eventually the examination that defines what is valued and dictates what must be taught.

Even with the optional procedure, the examinations as they are now designed are not fully consistent with the objectives of the new program. Until the Ministry of Education can develop examinations based on the new program, it is their policy to grant those schools that request it permission to set their own school-leaving examinations. Thus far, no school has exercised that option, most likely because there appear to be far too many inconsistencies between the notion of a set examination in English and current theoretical notions of how one might define achievement in language and literature and assess such achievement. Until examinations can be devised that take into account newer understandings of, for example, the relationships between reader and literary text, such examinations can only subvert the objectives of programs that build on such understandings. It is, in any case, government policy that, as more schools opt out of the traditional examinations set by the Ministry, examinations based on the new programs will be set by the Ministry and will become the norm rather than the exception. What must such examinations take into account? And how can they ensure that they do not undercut the new curriculum, that they not only support the new curriculum, but also help drive it? The discussion that follows explores these questions in the context of the teaching and examination of literature.

Examining Response to Literature

The program and the accompanying guides on the teaching of literature have attempted to move teachers away from the notion of literature as content to be handed over. The program works from

Rosenblatt's (1978) argument that the literary text is continually re-created in the transaction between reader and text, that the text is formed not only by the words on the page, but also by the experiences and expectations that the reader brings to the text. Moreover, the contexts within which the text is read also influence the nature of the literary transaction. Drawing from their responses, readers work to rely much more on their own resources as readers and to trust their own experiences of the literary work. Moreover, classroom contexts should encourage readers to become aware of possibilities of meaning (value tentativeness), to become tolerant of ambiguity, and to become unafraid of being wrong. Such contexts should encourage an "aesthetic" rather than an "efferent" stance, to use Rosenblatt's terms; they should promote exploration, a dwelling on the experience of the poem rather than an immediate search for the one right meaning. The program does not explicitly state such concerns; rather, the concerns derive from the theoretical principles that direct the program. What is explicit, however, is an insistence that all acts of communication occur within specific communication contexts and that it is the specifying of real, "meaningful," and challenging contexts in all language arts activities that will help develop students' competencies as users of language.

Given such concerns and recognitions, the difficulties of aligning the literature examination with the program objectives seem almost insurmountable. Even less certain seems any likelihood that the literature examination will "drive" the curriculum. It is now a commonplace notion that the situational context powerfully influences reading and writing. Where a text is read or written (at home or in a classroom), when (in a stressful situation or during one's leisure time), why (for pleasure, information, or a test), and for whom (teacher as examiner or sympathetic listener, oneself, or a friend) determine to a great extent what one derives from one's reading and the kind of writing one produces. Can an examination situation allow for the kinds of reading (and writing about one's reading) that the program objectives are set to promote? The testing of one's ability to read and make sense of a poem, for instance, sets off expectations and demands that affect considerably one's experience of the poem. Such a test situation typically calls for well-formed responses with teacher-examiner demands in mind and is unlikely to encourage in the student an aesthetic, responsive stance open to possibilities of meaning and receptive to personal associations. Surely it is the latter way of reading that one wants to validate through an examination.

I must remind readers that I am not about to make a case for the usefulness of examinations in English. My own inclination is to ask why one's reading of literature should be tested in any case, especially when such testing can easily be damaging to the delicate network of feelings and motives that energize aesthetic reading. However, given the reality of a system of public school-leaving examinations, one must work to ensure that such examinations do the least possible amount of damage to the objectives of the program and, where possible, support those objectives. It is important to remember, on the other hand, that the program is an existing reality as well and that it is the examination that must conform to the demands of the program. While a few members of the evaluation branch of the Ministry of Education expressed concerns derived from the sentiment, "if we can't test it, it's not worth teaching," such considerations were not allowed to prevail in the designing of the program. Those proposing them had to be satisfied with minor modifications in phrasing that do not affect the substance of the document. Thus, though the "testability" of the objectives was not a predominant issue at the time when the program document was drafted, the school-leaving examination requirement necessitates that the issue be resolved (without compromising the program objectives).

What Do We Evaluate?

Given the objectives of the program, what do we hope to evaluate when we evaluate response to literature? We are obviously not concerned with measuring readers' responses against a standard desired response (however such an account may be derived), though we recognize that some responses demonstrate a much fuller realization of the literary text than do others and are more attentive to the text and its possibilities of meaning. Should we say that as evaluators we attend to readers' responses not as end products of a literary transaction but as pointers to the nature of that transaction, to the kind of reading that has occurred?

We may have some idea of which directions to proceed in if we consider how we go about evaluating students' writing. We do not, for instance, posit an ideal written text against which student writing is measured. We are concerned primarily about the integrity of the student's text: how it hangs together, the nature of the writer's undertaking, and the degree of commitment to that undertaking.

These are rather vague criteria and open to widely differing applications; however, Wilkinson et al. (1980), in their elaborations of the dimensions (cognitive, affective, moral, and stylistic) along which language development can be assessed, demonstrate that such assessment is not only workable but necessary as well.

The difficulty with assessing literary response lies not only, and not even primarily, in determining the criteria to be applied in such assessment. Such work could begin with assembling representative samples of responses to several literary texts and having a team of readers test out schemes for assessing these responses. Even after a workable scheme has emerged, the question remains: how do we ensure that the responses being assessed approximate a full and true account of a reader's transaction with the literary work? Maybe the question is phrased too ambitiously. Full and true accounts of one's response are hard to come by even under optimum conditions. One might more realistically ask, how do we create, within examination contexts, the conditions that allow students to respond truly and fully to literary texts?

Contexts for Examining Responses to Literature

It is such questions that help induct public examinations in the service of good classroom practice. If we specify the examination contexts within which students' responses (as recorded or reported) can be more fully reflective of their transactions with literary texts, we are suggesting as well that such conditions must obtain in the classrooms that prepare them for these examinations. Just as the optional procedure in the composition examination I referred to earlier forced many teachers to incorporate into their teaching of writing some form of draft/discuss/revise procedures, it is quite likely that the contexts we specify for the literature examination will alter the classroom situations within which literature is read and taught.

Let us assume that we expect to test a reader's ability to call on and develop his or her own responses to literary texts and organize them to meet the demands of a critical examining audience. An examination based on such expectations should specify contexts which allow readers to do the following:

1. develop and elaborate on their responses to the text, and, to that end, engage in free and undirected discussion;

2. adopt an exploratory stance open to possibilities of meaning and tolerant of ambiguity;

3. take account of and recognize the value of personal experiences in the discovery and formulation of meaning; and

4. be willing to postpone closure, the settling on a final meaning.

Obviously such contexts do not ensure that readers will adopt the appropriate stances. These are attitudes toward reading literature that must be engendered in classrooms over a considerable period of time if they are to take. As I indicated earlier, the practices that help develop such attitudes are implicit in the stated objectives of the program. I have in mind here especially the collaborative reading and discussion that is called for in much of the discussion of the program objectives. The hope is that students will come to the examination with some degree of confidence in their ability to make sense of a literary text and will articulate their thoughts in a coherent and organized fashion for a critical audience. We may also assume all too easily that the literary text will somehow "take." But there are failed readings just as much as there are failed writings. Somehow the reader must draw on an appropriate context of feeling and information. Much will depend on how the examination assignment is drawn up and on the reader's degree of confidence that the text will eventually make sense.

A Proposal for a Process-Based Examination

What follows is an outline of a proposal for an examination in English, one of several proposals to be pilot-tested in 1986–87. The examination tests both composition and literature. The proposal assumes that the examination will occur over a period of several days and in a setting that is familiar and supportive. It is also assumed that students are accustomed to working in small groups and sharing their responses and their written drafts for comment and revision. The activities are listed below in order; how much time will be allotted to each activity has yet to be determined. Specific texts are identified and tasks described in order to give readers some sense of the demands of the various tasks and to justify the sequence.

Day 1

Part 1

Students are invited to recall an experience in which they were taught a skill or a lesson by a parent, grandparent, older relative, or acquaintance but did not recognize the value or importance of the skill or lesson to themselves or to the person who taught them. Only with the passage of time and in the light of further experience or a specific incident have they realized what they really learned.

Alternate Part 1

Students are invited to recall their early memories of a parent or elderly relative or acquaintance in the light of their present view of that person.

They should take note of their feelings, attitudes, and incidental details as these are recalled and use these notes to write an account that would be appropriate for a personal journal entry approximately 250–300 words in length.

Part 2

Students share their writing in groups of three and, if necessary, revise what they have written in the light of comments from the group. Both draft and final versions are handed in to the supervisor for inclusion in individual student folders.

Day 2

Part 1

1. The class is divided into groups of four or five.
2. Copies of the poem "Follower" by Seamus Heaney are distributed. (The speaker in the poem recalls his childhood admiration for his father as the father ploughed a straight furrow, and he marks the present reversal of roles as it is now the aged father who stumbles in the wake of his child.)
3. The teacher reads the poem aloud, or, as a worthwhile alternative, students in groups develop a reading of the poem and nominate a representative to read the poem aloud. Students note down initial reactions: feelings, observations, associations.
4. Students reread the poem silently and note further responses. One member in each group volunteers to read the poem aloud. Additional observations are noted.
5. *In turn*, members of the groups share their initial observations. Students do not comment on one another's observations until all members of the group have spoken. They may note down ideas

suggested to them by the observations of the other members of the group.

6. After this initial round of sharing responses, students comment freely on the poem with the intention of arriving at some consensus on what is happening in the poem.

Part 2

Preferably, part 2 is done after a short break of fifteen or twenty minutes, during which time students are free to continue talking about the poem.

Students (at their own desks) reread the poem silently in the light of the discussion that has occurred, make additional notes if necessary, and select what they consider to be the five aspects of the poem's meaning and form that are central to their understanding. Using these five items as a guideline, they then write a 200- to 300-word account of the poem meant to inform a reader at their grade level who has just completed one reading of the poem. These accounts, together with the notes from their discussions, are collected by the supervisor and placed in students' individual folders.

Day 3

Part 1

Students do steps 1–6 as outlined for Day 2 above. The poem to be read and discussed is Dale Zieroth's "Father" (1975). (The poem is again an adult's recalling of childhood experiences of his father in relation to the son's present view of him. Theodore Roethke's "My Papa's Waltz" is also useful in this context. I do not believe female students are particularly disadvantaged by the fact that the writers of these particular selections are male and write about male parents.)

Part 2

After a short break, students return to their individual desks, reread the poem silently, and record additional observations. Then, using their notes from the group discussion, they write in note form an account of the poem that includes their understanding of it and tells how the poem's language and form work to support that understanding. Both notes from the group discussion and individual accounts are added to the students' folders.

Day 4

1. Folders with copies of poems and notes are returned to students.
2. Students are invited to identify a common theme that underlies both poems and write a 300-word essay in which they compare and contrast the two in order to explore how the poems deal with the theme they have identified. Essays are placed in folders and returned to the supervisor.

Day 5

Part 1

Students follow steps 1–6 as set out for Day 2 above using "A Secret Lost in the Water" by Roch Carrier. (This [very] short story provides a moving account of a writer's realization of his dead father's true wisdom and skill.)

Part 2

Students return to their groups (preferably after a short break) to discuss these questions: Is it inevitable that at some time in their development children will reject or downplay the instruction or wisdom of a parent (or parental figure)? And is it just as inevitable that parents as they age will falter in the footsteps of their children?

Students take notes in preparation for an essay on a related topic to be written the next day.

Day 6

Students are given the following instructions. Their folders are at hand.

> You have been invited to speak to a small group of elderly people at a retirement home on the topic, "Will children always be (or think they are) wiser than their parents? And if so, how must we learn to live with this fact?"
>
> Write an essay (400–500 words) in which you present your point of view, taking into consideration your own experience, some of the readings you have done these past few days (you may assume that your audience is familiar with these readings), and some of the plays, novels, and films you recall which might touch on this theme. Submit all drafts to your supervisor with the other materials in your folder.

Commentary

A few notes are in order:

1. The procedure for the discussion of the poem and a rationale for the procedure are discussed in some detail in Dias (1979; 1985) and Bryant (1984).

2. As 50 percent of the final grade is based on work done during the year, teachers can be advised to provide for some writing on drama and the novel during the year.

3. The suggested number of words for the writing is intended only as a guide for the teacher. Students should at all costs be discouraged from slipping into a product-oriented, word-counting frame of mind.

4. The folders should be assessed as a whole. Criteria for assessment should be settled on only after a team of teachers has considered several representative folders.

The sequence of tasks is offered as a working model of an approach that attempts to deal with the difficulties of testing response to literature within the context of school-leaving examinations. A basic assumption is that students cannot be expected to respond to literature and write about their responses on command without reverting to formulaic writing and the manipulation of familiar terminology and clichés of literary criticism. The sequence of tasks and the days allotted for these tasks are intended to allow for a more considered, developed response. The preliminary recall exercise is intended to help ease students into the examination context with an assurance that their experiences are valued and worth writing about. Moreover, the task helps readers call up experiences that have some bearing on the literary texts they are about to consider. I do not believe the task directs their reading of the poems and the story in any particular way, and if it does, I expect the price is worth paying if it makes the passage into the reading of the poem less difficult. From the pilot testing I have done of this sequence, I must say that the students felt that the writing task had made them more sensitive to what was occurring in the poem.

There are some difficulties that cannot be ignored:

1. We cannot ensure that all small groups afford equal opportunities to their members in helping develop and clarify their responses to a work. We can but hope that teachers will recognize the need to have so incorporated small-group work into

their regular activities that no one group affords special opportunities to its members. This is another case of the test driving the curriculum.

2. We must recognize that there will be individuals who are unable to function productively in groups and who should therefore not be forced by the format of the examination into working in a style that does not suit them.

3. We need to be concerned about the quality of supervision; it should create a supportive climate and not distract.

4. Students will need to become accustomed to responding freely in writing. There is some evidence that students' written reports of their responses to a literary work may not adequately represent their actual responses and may actually mask real ability (Travers 1982).

Whatever anomalies one might detect in the examination procedures I suggest, I can still insist that the procedures dictate classroom contexts and practices that are consistent with current understanding of the relationship between a reader and a literary work and of how such transactions may be made available to other readers.

Acknowledgments

I must acknowledge here my debt to John Gaw and Marjorie Gawley of the Ministère de l'Education, Quebec, who convened the several committees that contributed to the development of the Quebec secondary language arts program and the program guides and who ran interference in the Ministère for the several radical recommendations emanating from these various committees. The views expressed here are the author's and should not be attributed to the Ministère.

References

Bryant, C. 1984. Teaching Students to Read Poetry Independently: An Experiment in Bringing Together Research and the Teacher. *The English Quarterly* 17 (4): 48–57.

Carrier, Roch. 1980. A Secret Lost in the Water. In *The Penguin Book of Canadian Short Stories*, edited by Wayne Grady. Harmondsworth, England: Penguin Books.

Dias, Patrick. 1979. Developing Independent Readers of Poetry: An Approach in the High School. *McGill Journal of Education* 14: 199–213.

———. 1985. Researching Response to Poetry—Part I: A Case for Responding Aloud Protocols. *The English Quarterly* 18 (4): 104–18.

Heaney, Seamus. 1968. Follower. In *Voices: The Third Book*, edited by G. Summerfield. Harmondsworth, England: Penguin Books.

Ministère de l'Education, Quebec. 1982. *Secondary School Curriculum: English Language Arts I–V.*

Rosenblatt, Louise. 1978. *The Reader, the Text, the Poem: The Transactional Theory of the Literary Work*. Carbondale, Ill.: Southern Illinois University Press.

Travers, D. M. 1982. Problems in Writing about Poetry and Some Solutions. *English in Education* 16 (3): 55–65.

Wilkinson, A., G. Barnsley, P. Hanna, and M. Swan. 1980. *Assessing Language Development*. Oxford: Oxford University Press.

Zieroth, Dale. 1975. Father. In *Mirrors: Recent Canadian Verse*, edited by Jon Pearce. Toronto: Gage Educational.

5 Imaginative Investigations: Some Nondiscursive Ways of Writing in Response to Novels

Peter Adams
Bauksia Park High School
Bauksia Park, South Australia, Australia

Peter Adams begins his essay with the question, What is lost if students are allowed to respond to literature only discursively? He answers with a demonstration of what is gained by offering students the opportunity to write from within the world of the text, a task which itself commits the students to a different mode of thinking (and a different use of language). When students write in this way, they are able to articulate responses to the literature—perceptions, feelings, insights—which draw upon intuitive or tacit levels of understanding and which do not readily lend themselves to formulation in discursive modes of writing, such as the literary critical essay. To demonstrate the power of this approach with a wide range of students, he pairs the writing (drafts and final versions) of two very different students, one who imaginatively reconstitutes a gap in *A High Wind in Jamaica* and another who writes an epilogue to *Lord of the Flies*. Through images, metaphors, and symbols, each student brings into focus aspects of the characters' experiences that are implicit in the novel, though not directly addressed by it.

The British educator and writer Peter Abbs recently began a review article with the following observations:

> We have as a civilization tended to confine intellectual meaning to linguistic forms and, furthermore, to those linguistic forms which are discursive in nature. . . . As a result of this preconception, other forms of intellection, through metaphor, through analogy, through dance, through colour, through the sequencing of sound, are seen as largely irrelevant. . . . This profound bias explains why the arts are often taught discursively [and] why the teaching of literature is conducted through endless discursive essays: essays which explain, give evidence and rationally defend a set position with a series of arguments. . . . The monopoly in educational practice of discursive reasoning

has led to a contraction and distortion so commonplace that it is
difficult to see, difficult to locate all that had been excluded.
(1984, 90)

While the teaching of literature has changed in ways that Abbs is
apparently unwilling to acknowledge in this context, his remarks
raise very clearly some of the questions with which I shall be concerned in this chapter. What is lost—excluded or neglected—if
teachers only make available to students discursive modes of response to the literature they meet in our classrooms? What kinds of
writing encourage nondiscursive modes of response? What happens
when students are allowed to reflect upon the literature they've
read, exploring its significance to them, through such kinds of writing?

As a way of beginning to address these questions, I want to focus
initially on one novel, one fifteen-year-old boy, and two pieces of
his writing. The novel is *A High Wind in Jamaica* by Richard Hughes,
and the two pieces of writing are both explorations of the episode in
which Margaret Fernandez takes up residence in Otto's cabin. Although the novel is well known, it will prove useful to recall the occasion in some detail.[1]

When Jonsen, the pirate captain, and his drunken crew made
their way down into the children's quarters in the forehold, it was
Margaret, the oldest, who most clearly understood the nature of the
danger she and Emily were in, even though it was Emily who re-
pulsed the intended assault by biting the captain's thumb. Margaret's subsequent behavior, however, remained incomprehensible
to the rest of the children (page numbers refer to the 1967 Panther
edition):

> For some time she had behaved very oddly indeed. At first
> she seemed exaggeratedly frightened of all the men: but then
> she had suddenly taken to following them about the deck like a
> dog—not Jonsen, it is true, but Otto especially. Then suddenly
> she had departed from them altogether and taken up her quar-
> ters in the cabin. The curious thing was that now she avoided
> them all utterly, and spent all her time with the sailors: and the
> sailors, for their part, seemed to take peculiar pains not only not
> to let her speak to, but not even to let her be seen by the other
> children.
> Now they hardly saw her at all: and when they did she
> seemed so different they hardly recognized her: though where
> the difference lay it would be hard to say. (91)

Immediately thereafter, the novel affords us a couple of revealing
glimpses of Margaret. When Emily was injured by the marlin-spike,
it was Jonsen who sprang to her aid

. . . and carried her, sobbing miserably, down into the cabin.
There sat Margaret, bending over some mending, her slim
shoulders hunched up, humming softly and feeling deadly ill.
"Get out!" said Jonsen, in a low brutal voice.
Without a word or sign Margaret gathered up her sewing
and climbed on deck. (104)

Where Margaret goes, we are not told, but she is the first on the
scene after Emily has murdered the Dutch captain, and the change
that has taken place in her is frightening:

[T]he first witness of the scene was Margaret, who presently
peered down from the deck above, her dulled eyes standing out
from her small skull-like face. (110)

To the returning pirates, of course,

It was plainly Margaret who had done it—killed a bound, de-
fenceless man for no reason at all; and now sat watching him
die, with her dull meaningless stare. (111)

The retribution that follows is swift and terrible:

She was lifted by the arms from the stair where she still sat, and
without a moment's hesitation (other than that resulting from
too many helping hands) was dropped into the sea.
But yet the expression of her face, as—like the big white pig
in the squall—she vanished to windward, left a picture in Otto's
mind he never forgot. She was, after all, his affair. (112)

The episode does not end there: Margaret is picked up by the second boatload of pirates returning from the Dutch captain's vessel
(they know nothing of what has gone on), and once back on board,
she

went straight forward as of old, climbed down the ladder into
the forehold and undressed, the other children watching her
every movement with an unfeigned interest. Then she rolled
herself in a blanket and lay down. They none of them noticed
quite how it happened: but in less than half an hour they were
all five absorbed in a game of Consequences. (113)

The episode is recounted in such a way as to raise insistently
those very questions which it refuses to answer—except with the
utmost obliquity. Why, we wonder, did Margaret's intense fear of
the sailors give way to fascinated interest? What wrought the terrible change in her appearance that we notice when she emerges from
her hiding place? What expression did Otto see on her face as she
disappeared overboard? And so on. Characteristically teasing and
enigmatic, the text prompts the reader into supplying what Emily

cannot supply and what the gnomic reticence of the narrator *will* not. What the text implies is that there is a point of view, not Emily's and not the narrator's (since he deliberately assumes the limited view of the participants), from which the whole episode will reveal its meaning. As Wolfgang Iser (1980) puts it:

> What is missing . . . stimulates the reader into filling the blanks with projections. He is drawn into the events and made to supply what is meant from what is not said. What is said only appears to take on significance as a reference to what is not said. . . . But as the unsaid comes to life in the reader's imagination, so the said "expands" to take on greater significance than might have been supposed. (110–11)

Discursive and Imaginative Responses

Iser's statement leads us directly to Robert's first piece of writing:

> When Margaret took up her sleeping quarters with Otto, she took a step into a kind of adulthood, leaving her childhood behind her. This step, she thought, would be good, in that she was separating herself from the rest of the children, and it was a sort of "growing up," leaving the others behind. But this "good step" was to turn out to be a tragic step, and Otto continued to use her—she had started to earn a reputation from the captain, and probably the other sailors, as a slut or a tool that was used by Otto. She was no longer that innocent inquiring little girl, and how she learned to *miss* that innocence.
>   When she looked down through the skylight of the cabin and saw the tragic thing Emily had committed, the murder of the Dutch captain, I bet she felt like weeping for the end of innocence, like the boys in the *Lord of the Flies*, weeping for the end of innocence for *Emily and* herself. First, Margaret lost her innocence of childhood through intercourse—then Emily lost her innocence of childhood through murdering the Dutch captain. Which sin was worse for a child, I have no idea!
>   As she was dropped overboard into the sea, I think the face Otto may have seen was the face of an indignantly hurt child. A *child*!
>   When she took up sleeping with the other kids again, she was trying to take a step backwards to childhood again—but it isn't at all successful, as the others isolate her and she can't have her innocence again, once she has lost it.

Whatever one makes of this (and it seems to me to be very uneven), it could hardly be said to prepare us for what was to come the following night, when Robert again took up the problem of Margaret's suffering:

Margaret sat on the bunk, gently rocking from side to side with the head swell, a downcast look on her face. She never ever really got sea-sick, but right now she felt decidedly queasy. As the stern once again shot into the air, and her stomach was forced down into her boots, the boat gave a melancholy sigh. Then, as the stern plunged down again and her stomach was eerily transported from her toes to her ears, she felt sure she was going to be sick.

It was dark in the cabin, and musty too, but the sun was shining outside. She could see the light coming through the crack in the door. The thin sliver of light pierced the darkness of the cabin, and she reached out and put her hand through it. It felt warm, which made her realize she felt cold. She wished that she could go out onto the warm deck. But she remembered what Otto had told her, and she knew, of course, why she wasn't allowed to go on deck with the other children.

With that idea gone, she turned her attention to the doll lying on the bunk beside her. She had made it from a rum bottle and wrapped some old rags around it. Onto the neck of the bottle she had pushed a large potato (which she had scavenged from the galley) and had pushed some splinters into it to serve as eyes and a mouth. Otto called it her "spud-head", but she called it "my child" and nursed it as if it were. Right now, her thoughts wandered over her own lost childhood, and she found herself absent-mindedly nibbling the doll's head with her neat fine teeth. Raw potato wasn't that bad.

As Otto opened the door and stepped in, she was suddenly brought back to the present.

"Get up," he said to her, and then sat on the bunk, and she stood up and went over to the door and, with one arm holding the doll to her chest, she ran her fingers down the crack where the sunlight was shining through.

"Come here," Otto said, and she turned to see him starting to undo the buttons on his shirt. Margaret turned back to the doll and started rocking it. She looked up at the roof of the cabin, where patters of little feet and squeals of delighted laughter showed that the children were engaged in their endless game of Consequences. She turned her back to Otto and looked at her feet, the laughter of the children echoing in her head.

"Come here." Otto's voice was flat and peremptory.

Margaret shook her head and bit her lip, still with her back to Otto.

"Hey?" he said, a little puzzled. "Come here." The children's laughter reached Margaret's ears again, then a single tear splashed on her foot. Her frail body was shaken by a wracking convulsive sob, and the doll fell, hitting the floor and breaking off at the neck. The potato head rolled up to Otto's feet and lay there, looking up at him.

This is, surely, a remarkably impressive piece of writing from a fifteen year old, and even on a first reading, we are aware that it embodies an understanding of Margaret's plight—grasped and presented in all its painful actuality—that is more searching and more sustained than he could manage in the first piece. Why?

Accounting for Differences

We might begin to account for the differences between Robert's two essays by noting that the whole thrust of the second piece is away from the discursive statement of meaning and towards its evocation through *poetic* means: through image, metaphor, and symbol. Even what Robert borrows is transformed in this direction. Hughes's apparently casual remark that Margaret was feeling "deadly ill" is taken up in Robert's opening and developed in such a way that one world, the objective world of the violently heaving cabin in which Margaret is sitting, becomes a metaphor for another, the inner world of psychological dislocation and disorientation in which the girl now finds herself. This is a world she is powerless either to escape or alter—like the ship itself, whose melancholy sigh, as it is heaved sickeningly from stem to stern on the head swell, seems an expression of the resigned weariness with which it too is compelled to endure what it cannot change.

Later in Robert's story, when the connections with the earlier piece of writing seem most apparent, we in fact have a particularly clear example of what it means to think *poetically* and of the greater precision and subtlety of thought this makes possible. The children's laughter overhead obviously represents the world of childhood experience that Margaret has forfeited, but childhood evoked now not as some prelapsarian state of grace ("She was no longer that innocent inquiring little girl, and how she learned to *miss* that innocence") but in terms of particular ways of feeling and being. What is evoked through the image of the children at play is the untroubled gaiety of childhood, its heedless freedom, and (perhaps most poignantly for Margaret) its capacity for self-forgetfulness. The gain in specificity is also a gain in precision of thought. Moreover, as she listens to the laughter, there seems to be no yearning for that lost world—the sounds of the children's play serve only to emphasize her own contrasting condition of misery and helpless entrapment.[2]

This image, furthermore, has its place in a larger pattern of images. In the contrast between the upper world of sunlight and warmth in which the children are absorbed in play and the lower depths in which Margaret is confined—cold, dark, and musty—our sense of Margaret's plight is deepened and intensified. She seems, in the gloomy underworld of the cabin, to have entered a world "where there is neither sense of life or joys" (Clare 1967) but only helpless suffering and a despairing consciousness of being set apart (forever, it seems) from the stir and warmth of the living human world. For Margaret, the "game of Consequences" is indeed "endless" and no game at all.

But it is the doll, of course, and the complex and subtle symbolism that is developed around it, that represent Robert's most brilliant intuitive stroke. Even if, as seems likely, Robert unconsciously took his cue from Rachel, who obsessively secreted her bundles of rags in odd places all over the ship, the use he makes of Margaret's doll is strikingly original and powerful.[3]

As she nurses the doll, Margaret is, of course, both mother and child. In this way, she is able not only to become again the child she once was but, at the same time, to experience the security and protectiveness of that maternal love whose present need she feels with such desperate urgency. But, if the doll represents a defense against those feelings of helplessness and vulnerability with which her circumstances fill her, it is a fragile defense, threatened both from within and without.

The inner threat comes in a moment of nostalgic reverie, when Margaret finds herself "absent-mindedly nibbling the doll's head." Ironically, in attempting, through the primitive psychological mechanism of incorporation, to recover what she has lost—the unspoilt childhood represented by the doll—she does to the doll what, just as unwittingly, she has done to her own childhood: under the influence of one compulsion, the doll is defaced, just as, under the influence of another equally gnawing compulsion, her childhood was marred.[4]

But the greatest threat, of course, is the external one, the threat represented by Otto. "Come here," he says, and Margaret begins to rock the doll in a desperate attempt to reassure herself that all will be well, that she is safe cradled in her own arms. But Otto's words drive a wedge between her and the doll, for they brutally recall her to an awareness of what she now is, just as the children's laughter, which echoes so poignantly and maddeningly in her head, reminds her of what she once was. In the contempt with which he treats her, in the brutal directness of his demands, in the complete absence of any shame or guilt on his part, she sees what she has become, and she is powerless to protest or resist. She is, after all, a child who has belied her childhood. The slow-thinking puzzlement with which

Otto greets her small show of defiance serves only to tell her how finally she has forfeited her right to be more than a passive and unre-
sisting instrument of his will.

When the doll smashes on the cabin floor, not only does its destruction recapitulate Margaret's original "fall," it also signals, in a
strikingly dramatic way, the final collapse of the defense mechanism
by which she had sought to protect herself against the psychological
threat represented by Otto. Nothing could more powerfully focus
her helpless vulnerability than the image with which Robert's story
ends.

Specifying the Tacit

It is clear, I think, that very little in Robert's first piece of writing
comes near to the sustained subtlety and complexity of his second
vision of Margaret's plight, and this was something of which Robert
himself was very much aware. In a conversation I had with him
some time after he had written the second of the two pieces, he
began and ended the interview by trying to formulate his sense of
their differences:

> RP: With this one [indicating the first piece of writing], I'm trying to ex-
> plain how she feels and why it happened, whereas with this one
> [indicating the second piece of writing], I can show it and I can ex-
> press it in other ways, other than having to write it down in actual
> words, and choose the words. I can show it in her actions, and the
> other people's actions, and the things that go through her head.
>
> PA: How did you feel when you finished the second piece?
>
> RP: As if [very expressively, with deep satisfaction], aah . . . you know?
> Um, how did I feel? Oh, very pleased with it, and that I'd stumbled
> across a lot of things I hadn't, I hadn't planned. Yeah, I, I was *very*
> pleased with it. It's not often I can . . . I mean, I like to sit down
> and write, and just write what comes, but this was a very suc-
> cessful one, I thought. When I finished, I thought, oh great, you
> know. It showed me lots of things that I thought, but couldn't write
> down as you see there [indicating the first piece of writing].

What is interesting about these remarks is the shift that has taken
place, during the course of our discussion, in Robert's sense of the
ways in which these two pieces of writing differ. At first, it is a simple matter of the difference between "telling" and "showing": the
labour of explicitness demanded by the discursive piece is con-
trasted with the concreteness of imaginative writing, where meaning
can be evoked in terms of "her actions, and the actions of other peo-

ple, and the things that go through her head." He speaks, that is, as if it is *the same kind of understanding* that seeks expression in both pieces of writing, and so, if the second piece is superior to the first, it would be because what he found difficult to state discursively, he has been able to convey successfully in the more congenial medium. While I do not wish to discount the difficulty of the kind of discursive writing he was attempting in the first piece, I think it is significant that, by the end of the interview, Robert sees the relationship between the two pieces of writing in a rather different light. The emphasis now falls upon what he has *learned* from writing the second piece: "It showed me lots of things I thought, but couldn't write down as you see there." He is pointing to the fact that writing like this exists not only to state things previously known or consciously grasped but also to embody perceptions and insights *at the point of discovery*.[5] He looks back on what he has written and realizes, with some surprise and a good deal of satisfaction, that it has been the means by which he has been able to articulate (and so become aware of) those intuitions, feelings, and ideas which were, in some sense, already *his*, but which could not have been elicited in any other way.

Most forms of writing, as we know, serve this heuristic function. As James Britton (1972) has pointed out, "We rarely use writing as mere communication. There is nearly always some element of exploration, of discovery, of finding out what it is we want to say." If this is true, to some extent, of *all* writing, then we need to ask why Robert got so much further in his second piece than he did in his first. We cannot simply pass his achievement off by saying that it represents the work of a remarkably gifted student. Rather, what we seem to have here is the work of an undoubtedly intelligent boy who is operating, in a memorable phrase of Jerome Bruner's, "at the far reach of his capacities." We need to know what has enabled this to happen. We can begin by listening carefully to what Robert has to say about writing the second piece:

PA: You'd written the first piece, then I'd asked you to try writing about Margaret as if you were the novelist trying to fill the gap in the book. How did you get started on the second piece of writing?

RP: Oh, well, I thought . . . I thought about, first of all, what got her in that position, so I had to bring that into it—you know, with Otto— and, um, I had to convey how she felt, by showing what she did— like, you know, with the light coming through, and she sort of passed her hand through and it felt warm, and it's like she's grasping for something there, the . . . the innocence, the warmth, and she felt cold. Um, I really started just by putting her in . . . you know, because she's always in that room . . . by starting off with, with her in the room and I, and I, I just wrote it, and thought about it in my mind, you know. I could see her getting up and I thought, now, what'd she do, you know, how would she act, if she felt that way, and that's basically how I got it.

PA: So what you're saying is that it wasn't planned out beforehand. . . .

RP: No, I didn't know how it was going to end.

PA: Were you surprised, when it was finished?

RP: Yeah, I . . . This bit here [indicating the last paragraph] . . . I could have left it with the bottle just breaking and smashing, and her looking at, in horror at it, but, but . . . so I just kept going and I thought, mmm, wouldn't that be great if the head just rolled up and looked at him, you know, and, er . . . and, er, it did surprise me, because . . . so, er, I just kept writing, a bit.

PA: So part of what you seem to be saying is that things you hadn't anticipated just arose . . .

RP: Yeah . . .

PA: And you'd think, hey, that's a . . .

RP: Yeah, that's how [indecipherable] it's meant to be happening.

. . . .

PA: So, you wanted an opening that was after the event, and that would show what? How she felt?

RP: Yeah, how she felt, mainly. That is, that's what I was trying to convey in everything, how she felt, and not just that, but how the situation was, not just how she felt, but how I felt about it.

PA: Can you tell me a bit more about that, because I don't think I understand that.

RP: 'Cause, well, showing what she did *is* how she felt, but that didn't have to happen there. That . . .

PA: Oh, the potato head rolling up to Otto's feet . . .

RP: And, and the stuff like that, that didn't have to happen.

PA: Is that showing how *you* felt?

RP: Yeah, I reckon it was . . . and, and a lit . . . and a little bit, I mean, not how *I* felt, but how I felt it would, er, bring Otto to a realization of what he's doing—not just Otto, but Margaret.

PA: Do you think Otto comes to a realization of what he's really doing to this little girl?

RP: I don't think he does, really.

PA: Do you think she realizes . . .

RP: It just confuses him, I think.

PA: Just confuses him?

RP: Yeah.

PA: Why, because first she comes to him and then she acts as if she doesn't want to continue this sort of relationship?

RP: Mmm, yeah. Mmm, confuses him that way. See, I said here . . .

PA: Yeah, "a little puzzled." Were you saying here, at the end, that

Margaret realized something about her situation that she hadn't known before, or what? I wasn't sure if you said that.

RP: Yeah, yeah, 'cause, she's like the child, right, she's like the child, and she's trying to nurture this child, but . . . bit late. And, um, when it broke and the head rolled up to Otto and looked at him, that's, that's like the child, breaking her childhood, and going to Otto, and it . . . she's broken herself, like a broken reed, you know.

PA: So, she can't ever get back to what she was?

RP: Yeah, that's right, she can't go back to innocence, childhood.

. . . .

PA: What made you think of the sliver of light coming in through the crack in the door?

RP: Well, that just sorta . . . I didn't really think of that, I just thought, right, she's sitting in the . . . she's sitting down. . . . I didn't plan it or anything, I just thought, she's sitting down there, and there's the door, and it wouldn't be totally dark, there'd be some light coming in somewhere, and I thought, you know, she'd be reaching . . . for light. She's in a . . . she's been in a dark, musty cabin, she'd go for light, you know . . . and I thought, coming through the door, 'cause it's a doorway . . . and, er, that's what mainly made me think of it.

PA: So it must have stood for a whole lot of things, that light?

RP: Yeah, it's . . . oh, I thought about it after I wrote it, that it did stand for heaps of things, not just for the one thing I wrote it. At the time I wrote it, I thought, in all this cold, she'd look for warmth, right, and after that I realized that it symbolized lots of other things too that, um, sh-, she's trying to . . . go back.

. . . .

PA: When she drops the doll and the head rolls up to Otto's feet, and lies there, looking at him, what seemed to you, when you were writing it, to have happened at that moment?

RP: Um, the thing that made it happen was, there's Otto, saying come here, with the children running above, she can hear the, you know, the innocent squeals of laughter and stuff, and the . . . Actually, she, she—where does it say?—she started to cry then, . . . "tear splashed on her foot," and, er, she started to cry and . . . it's because she could see what she *was*, and where she *is*—she's lost the innocence. She drops the foot at the moment she realizes . . . no, she drops the *doll* at that moment, 'cause she, 'cause she . . . She had to drop it there, where she realizes suddenly what has really happened. That's where she really realizes it, it really comes to her, and it falls and breaks and it's her, realizing she is broken.

A Radically Exploratory Investigation

Robert begins his conversation with me by speaking of having to convey *how* Margaret feels by showing *what* she does, but, as his subsequent remarks show, coming to decide what Margaret does is by no means a simple matter: "I could see her getting up and I thought, now, what'd she do, you know, *how would she act, if she felt that way*?" The scene has to be allowed, as it were, to declare its own direction: "I just thought, she's sitting down there, and there's the door, and it wouldn't be totally dark, there'd be some light coming in somewhere, and I thought, you know, she'd be reaching . . . for light." The significance of the light, what it symbolizes to Margaret, is apprehended directly—unmediated by abstract ideas—in terms of a pattern of sensuous contrasts: "She's been in a *dark*, musty cabin, she'd go for *light*, you know . . . in all this *cold* she'd look for *warmth*." (Significantly, even in retrospect, Robert cannot manage to adequately articulate what the light represents: "She'd be reaching for light, the . . . the innocence, the warmth.") Its meaning is intuitively grasped and, at the moment that its symbolic possibilities are glimpsed, what Margaret will *do*, the gesture that will reveal her feelings, proposes itself: "Yeah, that's how it's meant to be happening." The resulting gesture is felt to arise naturally out of Margaret's psychological situation at that moment and, in turn, achieves the revelation of feeling—or being—upon which he was intent.

But no such psychological necessity attends the moment in the story when the potato head rolls up to Otto's feet. In our discussion, Robert was at some pains to make this point: "Well, showing what she did *is* how she felt, but that didn't have to happen there. . . . I could have left it with the bottle just breaking and smashing, and her looking . . . in horror at it, but . . . I just kept on going and I thought, mmm, wouldn't that be great if the head just rolled up and looked at him." As with the sliver of light through which Margaret passed her hand, the meaning of this image is grasped intuitively and immediately, but (as Robert so acutely observes) it is prompted by a different necessity.

The image of the doll's head lying at Otto's feet and staring up at him in mute and inexpressive appeal captures both Margaret's inability to move Otto to an awareness of her plight and Otto's inability to even begin to imagine the depths of her suffering. It should, as Robert suggested, bring Otto to "a realization of what he's doing," but instead "it just confuses him." Otto lacks the capacity for imaginative insight needed to see that the doll *is* Margaret, just as he is unable to "read" Margaret's final anguished plea in the doll's unwinking gaze. To him, the doll is only her "spudhead" and nothing more, and it is precisely this kind of unimaginative stolidity that makes him so dangerous, for Margaret's "salvation" has now come to depend entirely upon his capacity to imaginatively enter into her world. Yet, at the same time as we see that, we also see that the broken doll *isn't* Margaret at all, but just a potato with some splinters pushed into it to represent eyes and a mouth. In other words, the image forces upon us a double vision in which the poignancy of Margaret's situation is intensified by our inability to apportion unequivocal blame.

Writing like this does not answer very well to conventional notions of the relationship between thought and language. Thought, as it exists in Robert's story, is neither prior to nor independent of its formulation in these particular images and symbols. What poetic modes of thought entail, first and last, is an effort of realization—an effort, that is, to imagine the given experience in all its vivid particularity—and in this effort of realization, of possession and creation, all the means by which we come to apprehend experience are brought into play: "blood, imagination, intellect running together." This entails a use of language that presents and enacts rather than states, language in which perception and feeling and insight are embodied in words that (as it were) speak for themselves. The meaning upon which the writer is bent is not something that is pursued abstractly or discursively, but in relation to experience that has itself been felt in all its fullness and directness. Thought is the presence, within this realizing activity, of an animating and controlling intelligence, alert to and quickened by its awareness of the significance that seems to be disclosing itself in and through these vividly grasped particularities—a significance which in turn guides the writer's further activity as he seeks to persuade it to elicit itself more fully. Poetic modes of thought, therefore, are not abstracted out from the specific weight, density, and texture of particular experience—the pressure of the actual. And so the meaning that the writer finds in this experience is not something that he has determined beforehand or imposed upon the material from outside but is something which is felt to arise from within the experience. It is not surprising that, in the end, the writer may not always be able to say *what* is the significance of what he has written, only that he knows it *is* significant. (In fact, when Robert handed me the second piece of writing, he said, with a grin, "It's got ironies in it even I don't understand.")

Robert's imaginative reconstruction of this particular gap in Hughes's text is the vehicle for a radically exploratory investigation of Margaret's plight, an exploration that not only draws upon kinds of intuitive or tacit understanding that do not readily lend themselves to discursive formulation but that constantly beckon him forward, toward "the far reach of his capacities."

The Far Reach of All Students' Capacities

As the interview suggests, Robert is a serious and thoughtful student who not only is a fluent and articulate writer, but also is capable of taking an unusually self-conscious interest in his own writing processes. Although *he* was surprised and delighted by his second piece of writing, we are perhaps not entirely taken aback by his success: at fifteen, he was sophisticated enough to have read *A High Wind in Jamaica* twice in quick succession because it piqued his interest. Are other students—those who are less articulate and less confident about themselves as writers—capable of writing in this sort of way? The answer, I think, is yes.

The following pieces of writing are by another fifteen-year-old boy. I had first taught Shane when he was in year 8, the first year of secondary schooling in South Australia. At that time, he was something of an isolate who came in for a good deal of teasing from the others in the class. His written work was chronically untidy, poorly spelled, and often suggested little real engagement with the task, although he would sometimes talk with enthusiasm about the stories he was writing in his journal. (This enthusiasm rarely sustained itself long enough for him to actually finish one of the wildly improbable space adventures upon which he had embarked.) Two years later, in year 10, he was much more isolated. He sat alone, took no part in class discussions, and avoided answering direct questions (for fear of drawing attention to himself, I suspect). His written work was scrappy and slight.

Towards the end of the year, I read *Lord of the Flies* with Shane's class, and after all the discussion that the book invariably generates, I asked the students to write an epilogue to the novel, in which they chose one of the survivors and showed how he reacted to being returned to "civilization" in England after his experiences on the island.

This is Shane's first draft of "After the Rescue":

RALPH

He sat on the porch in his chair, stairing out to sea at the battleships in deep thought. The ship that had brought him of the island 10 years ago ~~lay out~~ was mored in the harbour ~~and~~ All the thoughts of the islands came back to him, as though he was living the insident all over again and he couldn't take his mind of it, as though it haunted him and would keep haunting him ~~all his life~~ untill he died. ~~All the~~ Simon, and Piggy's death came to his mind and a quiver was sent down his back. All the bad things that went on on the island weren't suposed to happen to him but they did. He fell into a deep sleep as the ships pulled out of the harbour once more.

Reading that depressed me; all I could see were its inadequacies. Because the opening leaned so heavily on one of the examples I'd shown the class,[6] I didn't take much notice of the image of the battleships moored in the harbour (an image that not only persisted through the subsequent drafts, but developed in significance), nor did I notice the odd plaintiveness of that second-to-last sentence, with its unsettling hint at the unfairness of experience: what happened on the island wasn't supposed to happen to people like Ralph, but it did nonetheless. Instead, as I cast around for something positive to seize upon, I was struck by the rhythm of the last sentence and the (probably unintentional) parallel it suggested between Ralph falling asleep and moving out into the deeper waters of the unconscious and the battleships moving out of the comparative safety and calm of the harbour. So I suggested to Shane that he might want to develop this parallel and tell us what Ralph dreamed about while he was asleep. The next draft came to me in two installments, the first of which appears below:

RALPH

~~He sat on the porch in his chair, staring out to sea at the batle ships.~~

He sat on the porch in his chair, in deep thought, staring out ~~a~~ to sea. The ships that had brought him off the island ten years ago was moored in a small horse shoe shaped harbour with the outher battleships. All the ships from the small cruisers to the big battleships lay ~~mored~~ out in perfectly straight lines along the shore, one behind the other. All having a brightly painted British symbol on the side of the ships. Out beyond the ~~rest lay~~ masive ships lay 2 submarines, they were away from the rest and they stood out like. ~~like Jack and Roger standing out from the rest. His mind shifted drifting back. like~~ His thoughts changed for a moment. Like Jack and Roger standing out from the rest. ~~He~~ His eyes then focused back on the ships then to the beach were ~~20~~ twenty or ~~3~~ thirty small life rafts lay ~~on the sandy beach.~~

The heat of the day was slowly getting to him along with the sun in his eyes. He closed his eyes ~~in thought as the ships started to file slowly out the harbour.~~

~~The warmth comforted him as he dozed off to sleep~~ and fell into a deep sleep as the ships pulled out of the harbour once more.

What is most significant about this draft, I believe, is the analogizing habit of mind at work in it, for it allows Shane to draw upon things he understands about the novel but which he had previously been unable to bring into play. My specific suggestion about a parallel between Ralph falling asleep and the flotilla moving out of the harbour is less important than the possibility it opened up for Shane of exploring other parallels, some of which (perhaps) were implicit even in that first draft. Not suprisingly, some of the parallels (such as the two submarines) are stated rather obviously, but taken together, the promptings to recollection are varied and subtle. The way the ships are assembled in perfectly straight lines, "from the small cruisers to the big battleships," each with its "brightly painted British symbol," seems designed to make us think of the schoolboys and the unquestioned authority that prevailed among them while they were still in the world of the grown-ups. When Ralph's gaze shifts from the battleships to the "twenty or thirty small life rafts" lying drawn up on the sandy beach—a significant alteration of scale—we are reminded of the "littl'uns," who spent their days on the island playing contentedly in the shallows along the shore.

But the dominant impression created by this scene is of the immense power of the flotilla moored in the harbour, and, although it is presently at rest, we cannot help but be aware of its capacity for destruction once it has left the encircling embrace of the horseshoe-shaped harbour. (The fact that the scene specifically reminds us of what happened to the boys once they were away from a "civilization" that held their aggressive and anarchic impulses in check serves only to heighten the pervasive suggestion of menace.)

Shane waited for my response to this installment before, some days later, he went on to attempt the next section. (He was reluctant, perhaps, to move out into the uncharted waters of Ralph's dream without some reassurance.)

RALPH

Ralph starts dreaming about a ship that ~~he~~ is in his hands.

"Captain look, smoke." ~~to the~~

"Yes I see, Hand me my telescope and get the life raft ready to go ashore"

"Yes captain"

"Take me ashore, we wont need men, you wouldn't believe but its a bunch of boys"

"Yes sir, right away sir

"Look sir there a boys every where."

"Yes I can see"

"We had better get on with it"

"Are you coming ashore sire"

"Yes, I'm coming.

"Start the motor and take us in on shore now"

"Pull the boat up there on the beach"

"Sir the children are all painted and runing towards us with spears."

"Watch out lad, stretcher man wounded, go back to the life boats, don't shoot at them.

"To late sire, they have surrounded us."

"We want your Captain" said one of the savages.

They circled Ralph out and started chanting and jabbing him.

Ralph ~~awoke up~~ ~~in a~~ startled and in a hot sweat just to see the last smoke stack in the distance of the ships.

This draft has every sign of uncertainty, as if Shane recognized quite early in the piece that doing the dream like some kind of radio play was unsatisfactory ("Look sir there a boys every where." "Yes I can see") but was either unable to conceive of a better solution or was more concerned to get his ideas down on paper than he was with their most effective presentation. Not only is the form wrong, but much of the dialogue, too, seems to draw upon the conventions of third-rate TV dramas: lines such as "To late sire, they have surrounded us" or "We want your Captain" sound altogether too familiar.

I asked Shane to describe where Ralph was at the beginning of his dream and suggested that Shane would have to tell us about what happened in Ralph's dream—he couldn't rely on dialogue. The results can be seen in his next draft.

RALPH

He sat on the porch in his chair, in deep thought, staring out to sea. The ~~sips~~ ships that had brought him off the island ten years ago were anchored in a small horse-shoe shaped harbour with the other battleships. All the ships from the small cruisers to the big battle ships lay ~~moored~~ ~~better~~ at anchor in perfectly straight lines along the shore, one behind the other, all painted a dull gray.

Out beyond the massive ships lay two submarines. They were away from the rest and they stood out like . . . like . . . His mind seemed to reach for a thought, and then lose it. He looked back at the ships, then he looked down to the beach where twenty or thirty small life rafts lay.

The heat of the day and the sun in his eyes was making him lethargic. He fell into a deep sleep as the ships began to pull out of the harbour once more. Ralph began to dream . . . ~~an adventure.~~

Ralph was standing on the bridge, staring out to sea through his binoculars. ~~The sea was quite calm for this morning, thought Ralph, as his head swung round with the binoculars. What is.~~ There on the horizon was a thick acrid column of smoke belching up from nowhere. ~~They~~ He suspected it to be a burning ship ~~that~~ that had been bomed or had been torpedoed but he wasn't shore. They headed towards it and as they got closer they discovered that it was an island, not a burning ship. As they approached the island Ralph noticed ~~that~~ there were young boys on the beach playing. Ralph told his crew to put two life boats in the water and for five men and himself to go ashore and pick the young boys up.

As they landed in the life raft a group of boys came charging out of the brush and immediately surrounded Ralph. The boys started chanting and thrusting their spears at him. Out of the brush came four older boys carrying a chair on long poles. The boy that sat on the seat was holding a skull in his arms. The boy pointed the skull at Ralph and told the savages with spears to kill them. A savage raised his spear.

Ralph woke in a ~~deep~~ hot sweat ~~and as~~ just to see the last trail of smoke from the ~~ships~~ last ship.

This draft is much more assured and confident than any of the previous ones. It is neatly written in a cursive hand I didn't know Shane could command, and corrections are made with white correction fluid and carefully overwritten. The whole product suggests not only confidence, but an uncharacteristic pride in his work.

Some of the changes that appear in this draft are the result of suggestions I had made earlier. For instance, I had asked Shane what the "brightly painted British symbol" was, and his response (apparently) was to eliminate all reference to it, replacing it with something that suggests, in context, a sombre and unbeglamouring uniformity. Similarly, I had suggested to him that the link between the submarines and Jack and Roger was too obviously made, and the result is a subtler version of his earlier attempts to suggest the way in which Ralph's mind sought out the link with the past: "His mind shifted, drifting back/His thoughts changed for a moment. . . . like Jack and Roger standing out from the rest" has become "His mind seemed to reach for a thought, and then lose it." (We might say, by the way, that he has learned something of the value of the "blanks" of which Wolfgang Iser was speaking earlier in this chapter.) But the most significant alteration, of course, is to the dream, which has begun to assume its final form. After an initial false start with

Ralph's interior monologue, he settles down into past tense narration.

Shane's final draft followed shortly thereafter.

RALPH

He sat on the porch in his chair in deep thought, staring out to sea. The ships that could have brought them off the island ten years ago were anchored in a small horse-shoe-shaped harbour with the other battleships. All the ships, from the small cruisers to the big battleships, lay at anchor in perfectly straight lines along the shore, one behind the other, all painted a dull grey.

Out beyond the massive ships lay two submarines. They were away from the rest and they stood out like . . . like . . . His mind seemed to reach for a thought, and then lose it. He looked back at the ships, then he looked down to the beach where twenty or thirty small liferafts lay.

The heat of the day and the sun in his eyes made him lethargic. He closed his eyes as the ships began to pull out of the harbour. Ralph began to dream . . .

He was standing on the bridge, staring out to sea through his binoculars. There, on the horizon, was a thick acrid column of smoke, belching up from nowhere. He suspected it was a ~~burning~~ ship that had been bombed or ~~had been~~ torpedoed, but he wasn't sure.

They headed towards it and as they got closer he could see through his binoculars that ~~there~~ it was an island burning, not a ~~burning~~ ship. All he could see was the top of the mountain poking out of the smoke. As they approached the island, Ralph noticed ~~through his binoculars~~ that there were young boys on the beach, playing. He told his crew to put two lifeboats in the water. Five men and himself would go ashore and pick the children up.

As they landed in the liferaft, a group of boys came running out of the brush and immediately surrounded Ralph. The boys chanted and thrust their spears at him. He told the men to break their little sticks in half and so the men started to walk ~~inwards~~ forward. The men stopped, for out of the brush came four older boys, carrying a litter upon which was seated a red-haired boy. He was holding a skull in his arms. The boy pointed the skull at Ralph and spoke to the other savages. A savage raised his spear. . . .

Ralph woke up in a hot sweat, just as the last trail of smoke from the last ship disappeared below the horizon.

In some ways, Ralph's dream voyage to the island recapitulates his experiences ten years earlier. In the dream, the transformation of Ralph's vision of the boys (from children playing on the beach to savages with raised spears) parallels his journey in the novel from naive optimism to a grief-stricken awareness of "the darkness of man's heart." But there is a difference: in the dream, Ralph has identified himself with the naval officer who landed on the burning island, and what happens in the dream inverts the ending of the novel.

In the novel, the officer's arrival brought an abrupt shift in perspective: the "savages" suddenly became little boys again, and order and adult sanity effortlessly prevailed. But when Ralph orders his men to break the children's "little sticks," it is the signal for a chilling assertion of the reality of their identity as savages. No deus ex machina steps in at the end of this nightmare. Instead, Ralph wakes to see "the last trail of smoke from the last ship disappear below the horizon." The fear to which Ralph's dream testifies—that the adult world for which he stands in the dream is powerless either to reverse or control the savagery of the island—has found its confirmation in the waking world: while he was dreaming, the battleships have steamed out of the harbour, and Ralph wakes just at the moment that they slip beyond the possibility of recall. In both worlds, Ralph finds himself powerless to contain or prevent what his experience has taught him to fear most deeply. But it is not simply his own powerlessness as an individual that he has come to learn; the belief that dies in Shane's epilogue is the child's naive belief in the existence of a transcendent source of order and authority. And in this, Shane takes Ralph one decisive step beyond where Golding left him.

It is a sobering conclusion, but one that was implicit from the start. Through all the drafts, we watch Shane working out the implications of Ralph's feeling that the things that happened on the island "weren't supposed to happen to him, but they did," and in the process the plaintiveness disappears, to be replaced by a dry-eyed acceptance that the adult world affords no guarantees against the violence of the human heart.

These essays—Robert's and Shane's—are important, I believe, because they suggest what can happen when we allow our students to make "an 'artistic' response to the 'artistic' work of others." That formulation is not mine; it comes from an important section of Robert Witkin's *The Intelligence of Feeling* (1974), and I would like to end this chapter by quoting the passage in which it occurs, because it seems to me to be a central statement of the principles that should guide us in the encounters we arrange between our students and literature:

> Analysis and criticism [of literature] does have an important part to play in English studies, but it is in no way a substitute for,

nor is it synonymous with, creative appreciation. The latter requires that realized form be closely related to the pupil's creative expression and that he express his feeling response in a direct and personal way. It requires that he make an "artistic" response to the "artistic" work of others. (68)

Notes

1. A slightly different version of this material on *A High Wind in Jamaica* appears in Peter Adams's chapter "Writing from Reading—'Dependent Authorship' as a Response" in *Readers, Texts, Teachers*, edited by Bill Corcoran and Emrys Evans (Boynton/Cook, 1987, pp. 123–28). It is used by permission of the publisher.

2. The unconscious sexual symbolism of the crack in the cabin door serves not only to remind us of how Margaret entered this world, but, when she wistfully runs her fingers down it, the gesture subtly emphasizes the impossibility of return. (Her symbolic rebirth comes only after she has been cast overboard—out of death she wrings a provisional kind of restoration.)

3. Robert's comments on this are instructive:

PA: What made you think of the doll?

RP: Well, I thought, she, she's, um, she's fairly down, and she, she feels she hasn't looked after herself very well at all, and now with her, um, the doll, and I tried to make it, deliberately made it a bottle, a rum bottle.

PA: Go on.

RP: Something that Otto had been drinking from.

PA: Uh huh. . . . Why?

RP: Oh, it's like being . . . like right from the start, I suppose. It's like, it's like . . . . I don't know why, but, if you have the, um, bottle, that's been used by Otto, he's been drinking from it, and, rum, that's, that's often something that turns men, um, out of his senses. Um, um, if I m-, if I made the child like a temptation like rum. . . . It's something that's, you know, like a bottle there [reaching out with one hand towards a bottle imagined to be standing on the table in front of him] that hasn't been opened yet or something.

PA: But, of course, it's empty. . . .

RP: It is empty, yeah . . . um, and because it's empty, it's been used.

PA: It interests me that it has to be something of Otto's that she takes and transforms into an image or symbol of her own.

RP: Mmm. Yeah, well, I, I thought, she could take something of herself and . . . you know, a shoe or something like that. I thought about that, but, no, I thought it had to be something of Otto, had to have Otto in it.

PA: You didn't remember Rachel?

RP: [Silence]

PA: From the book?

RP: Mmm?

PA: And her dolls?

RP: Oh, about the way she went planting them all over the ship and stuff?

PA: Yeah.

RP: [Thoughtfully] No, I didn't think about that.

PA: You didn't remember this, from towards the end of the novel: "A cousin in England once sent them out some expensive wax dolls, but even before the box was opened the wax had melted: consequently the only dolls they had were empty bottles, which they clothed with bits of rag . . . "?

RP: [Surprised laughter] I didn't remember that at all! I didn't know that!

Robert's sense of it is that he worked his own way towards the symbol, and the references in the novel, if they entered into the process at all, did so unconsciously.

4. This was an irony of which Robert was very much aware:

PA: What made you think of having Margaret nibble the doll's head as her thoughts returned to her own past?

RP: I don't know what made me think of that, I just did it. Um, now where did I write it? Er, [reading] "her thoughts wandered over her own lost childhood . . . nibbling the doll's head." She lost her own childhood herself, didn't she? She did it herself. There she is nibbling away at the other doll, isn't she?

PA: I don't understand what you're telling me.

RP: She, she smashed it. Yeah, that's right. But, whereas, I'm trying to show that she, she did it herself, and here she is . . . here she is destroying the doll *absent-mindedly*. All that . . . there she is holding it and trying to look after it, and there she's nibbling at it. . . . And I thought she's, you know, she's sort of absent-mindedly doing something she wouldn't want to do . . . she's saying that she, she doesn't really mean to do it but when . . . it's subconscious, really.

5. As Barrett Mandel says, "Writing doesn't lay out the notions that are lying dormant in the mind waiting to be displayed. Writing is the 'seeing into' process itself. It is the tearing through the mind's concepts. The process itself unfolds truths which the mind then learns" (1978, 366).

6. One of the examples I had shown Shane's class was this epilogue, written by a year 10 student the previous year:

JACK

Jack sat in an old cane chair on the verandah of his beach shack. He looked down towards the beach and moved his eyes up to the horizon. The water was smooth and glassy and seemed to be repeating itself all the way to the skyline. His two children ran up to the steep winding path that led from the beach to the house. The youngest of them ran up to her father.

"Daddy, look what I found!"

She held a large shell in her outstretched hands.

"And Dad, if you hold it to your ear you can hear the sea."

She handed him the shell. Jack put it to his ear. He listened to the familiar echoing sound of air moving in and out of the shell—constant, peaceful, soothing—like water breaking on a distant reef, with the sound of the smaller waves lifting and dying on the sand.

Then, slowly and faintly, another sound appeared, just barely audible. The sound began to get louder, as if it was growing in the shell, starting from the middle and winding itself around the spiral cavity. After a few seconds he could recognize the sound: "Kill the beast! Cut his throat! Spill his blood!"

Jack began to shudder.

And out of the chant came the three most horrifying words Jack had heard on the island.

"I meant that!"

Jack began to cry.

References

Abbs, Peter. 1984. English and the Dynamics of Art-Making: A Review Article of *Learning through Writing*, Bernard Harrison (NFER). *English in Education* 18 (2): 90–96.

Britton, James. 1972. Writing to Learn and Learning to Write. NCTE Distinguished Lecture, Troy State College, April.

Clare, John. 1967. I am. In *Selected Poems and Prose of John Clare*, edited by Eric Robinson and Geoffrey Summerfield. Oxford: Oxford University Press.

Iser, Wolfgang. 1980. Interaction between Text and Reader. In *The Reader in the Text: Essays on Audiences and Interpretation*, edited by S. R. Sulieman and I. Crosman. Princeton, N.J.: Princeton University Press.

Mandel, Barrett J. 1978. Losing One's Mind: Learning to Write and Edit. *College Composition and Communication* 29:362–68.

Witkin, Robert M. 1974. *The Intelligence of Feeling*. Portsmouth, N.H.: Heinemann.

6 Novels: Vehicles for Time Travel for Middle School Students

Ben Brunwin
Laboratory School for the Academically Gifted
Chesapeake, Virginia, United States

Unlike the four preceding authors, Ben Brunwin does not make a case for a student-response curriculum, nor does he refer to this approach. He demonstrates its use instead by delineating a project for reading five novels with middle-grade students. He involves students in constructing a personal, imaginative experience based on the printed text. His imaginative framework for learning engages and motivates students to have a personal stake in the literature they read. Brunwin's account of a sample lesson meets many of the Dixon and Stratta criteria for character questions: the students' personal readings and interpretations are encouraged; students are asked to imagine their characters in action in encounters with other characters; they are invited to consider characters in specific scenes; and above all, students are encouraged to be involved in the characters' point of view, to empathize with them deeply, and to discover as *they* discover.

In teaching middle-grade students in England and fifth-grade students in the United States, I developed a method for teaching five novels that drew pupils imaginatively into the personal and historical worlds of the fifteenth to the twentieth centuries. The pupils were asked to take the central role in a learning journey, a magical adventure which was presented to them before they began reading. They were to delve into and voyage through the pages of five historical novels spanning six centuries.

In the role of Izzy Moonshine, a survivor of the nuclear holocaust of the twenty-first century, students travel through time and meet the central character in each of the five selected novels. They then "trade places" with the book characters in order to experience the worlds of the novels.

But placing students in a preestablished dramatic framework was not enough to engage them in the rich learning I envisioned. From the outset, students were given a clear direction and purpose, a motive with which they could readily identify and to which they could willingly relate. They were asked to enter their fictive worlds and compile insights into social conditions, class structures, individual behaviour, social relationships, and industrial developments. Thus they were invited to confront deeper, underlying key concepts of similarity and difference, continuity and change, cause and effect, independence and interdependence, conflict and consensus, power and communication, values and beliefs. As Izzy, the pupils were to encounter unexpected situations, develop initiatives, make decisions, form judgments, and solve problems—in fact, to exercise the widest range of intellectual skills.

The learning benefits of this model accrue to pupils and teachers alike. Pupils have a clear mission of discovery and, therefore, a relevance and meaning for their reading and subsequent research. Teachers can work with quality children's literature. The model offers possibilities for individual or team teaching in language arts or in integrated curriculum areas. It is a model which uses the power of empathy to enable children to project their personalities into a wide range of historical circumstances and so to develop a fuller understanding of fundamental issues in the human experience.

Implementation of the Project

The project has an impressive (and long!) title: "The Adventures of Izzy Moonshine, Traveller through Time: Transportation of Delight through the Imagery of Literature into Situations and Characters of Different Places and Times." The project was lodged under the umbrella of the "Industry through the Ages" unit. It was multifaceted and involved 120 children for about five hours per week over a period of eight weeks. Four teachers were permanently available for the project, and a fifth intermittently so. Five novels were chosen that were intrinsically worth reading. It was decided that each group of pupils should spend two weeks with each teacher on the book that had been chosen by that teacher. Pupils were therefore guaranteed extensive contact with at least four novels, and the teachers prepared material on the background of the books as well as on the books themselves. The following books were selected (all Penguin/ Puffin titles):

The Woolpack by Cynthia Hamett
The Iron Lily by Barbara Willard
Whistling Clough by Walter Unsworth
The Nipper by Catherine Cookson
The Incline by William Mayne

The project was launched through an imaginative framework that greatly appealed to the pupils. All of them were assembled to learn from a storyteller armed with enthusiasm and overhead projector transparencies about Izzy Moonshine. I include the gist of the story-teller's "script" below to make our work explicit and to provide a guide for a similar project. I have interspersed some comment about the instruction for which the story provided the imaginative frame-work. For one novel, *The Iron Lily*, I have given a more detailed ac-count of typical classwork.

The Script: Introduction of Izzy Moonshine, Son of Dr. Ziggy S. Moonshine, Child of the 2040s, Traveller through Time

The script goes something like this:

England in the twenty-first century presents a civilization which has survived the nuclear holocaust of the year 2000. However, hav-ing existed for a decade in a subterranean land of galleries below the earth's surface, humanity has returned to the surface of a planet de-void of face and feature, clad continually in highly insulated mate-rials in order to withstand the effects of radiation. Cultural records from throughout history have been erased in a single explosion; nothing remains as a record of our previous existence on this planet. For continuation and progress, humankind has been left totally de-pendent upon the knowledge and expertise of the band of survivors who step back up on the earth's surface in the year 2010.

Dr. Ziggy S. Moonshine is one of this band. A combination of his and his compatriots' inventive genius has produced a fully auto-mated civilization in England by the year 2040. Dr. Moonshine, at the age of eighty-six, was heralded by the New People, as the sur-vivors were now known, as the greatest inventor of their or any other time. *Time* was the key word in this recognition, for long be-fore people had mastered the knowledge of travel through the three dimensions, Izzy Moonshine's father had conquered the mysteries of travel through the fourth dimension, time.

The construction of the craft for this incredible journeying was completed, and all the New People awaited the announcement of its creator's decision on the choice of "aeonaut" and the times to be visited on the first voyage. When the announcement was made public, none could argue against the wisdom of the old man's decision. It had been the doctor's dearest wish that he himself should be the first ever "aeonaut," but he was forced to accept the realities of age and failing health which made this impossible; accordingly, he selected his son Izzy for the task.

The doctor's communication then explained the reasons for selecting those times to which Izzy would return. He explained how, without the use of materials created by five specific industrial processes, his invention would never have been possible. For this reason, the doctor expressed a deep feeling that both he and all the New People owed a debt to both history and the future to return in time and regain the lost insight and knowledge of the past that had led to producing the five refined materials on which the conquest of time hinged. He named the five materials to which he owed the possibility of his invention and the time channels to which the craft was to be programmed:

1. The entire interior of the time craft was fashioned in wool to provide both a maximum of warmth and of lightness. Thus, the wool trade of the fifteenth century was to be visited.

2. All instrumentation on the craft was of iron and steel, to furnish strength and sensitivity; therefore, the iron industry of the sixteenth century was programmed in.

3. The spherical exterior of the craft was formed of lead to achieve protection from heat and radiation; accordingly, the lead mines of the seventeenth and eighteenth centuries were included.

4. Power for the craft came from the explosion of a combination of coal gasses, so the coal mines of the nineteenth century were put on the list.

5. Finally, stone weights were built onto the ship to act as stabilizers and to offset the craft's natural rotational movements. Thus the last visit on the programme was to a stone quarry in the early twentieth century. [An illustration of the craft is provided on an overhead projector transparency.]

In conclusion, the doctor explained that to ensure that Izzy gained insight into the situations of the people he was studying, he would trade places with someone from the particular time and place he was visiting. Izzy would take with him quantities of gold (which had now been discovered in great plenty) to persuade suitable subjects to allow him to take their place. With the marvels of the cosmetics which had now been invented, Izzy would have no difficulty in changing his appearance to the exact double of the person of his choice. And his skill at mimicry would overcome any voice differences. Izzy would take with him a micro-camera and a cassette recorder, essential equipment for recording observations and experiences.

The Script Continues: The Voyage into Time

The day of the first voyage arrived, the preparations were completed, and Izzy stepped aboard the sphere. [Here the children are provided with an overhead projector illustration of Izzy.] With the all-clear light flashing, almost immediately the sphere began to rotate, ever faster, until the broken lines of an indistinct blur dissolved into nothingness. The journey had begun, and Izzy the aeonaut was slipping back through the centuries. [An overhead projector illustration of the craft's interior instrumentation is provided here.]

Inside the sphere, enclosed in a circular room of woolly warmth, Izzy was aware of only three sensations: the illumination of the blue all-clear light flashing, a certain light-headedness, and the subsequent illumination of the red channel-achieved indicator.

Stepping from the sphere, Izzy found himself on a grassy hillside with a hot sun beating down upon his head. He was immediately aware that he did not have the hillside to himself, for from all quarters he could hear the gentle bleatings of sheep grazing. Several yards above and ahead of him lay the prostrate form of a youth of his age taking shelter from the glare of the afternoon sun beneath the generous branches of an ancient oak tree.

Izzy's First Adventure: The World of "The Woolpack" by Cynthia Hamett

Izzy's adventures had begun. The youth's name was Nicholas Fetterlock [an illustration is provided], and he was the son and heir to Thomas Fetterlock, member of the Fellowship of Merchants of the Wool Staple and one of the richest wool merchants in the Cotswolds. The year was 1493 and the wool trade, then England's most important industry, was governed by three hundred leading wool merchants, who had the headquarters of their organization located in Calais. Known colloquially as "the Staple," they fixed and controlled the price of wool and made the rules for anyone in the trade. To be a member of the Staple was a very high position, and Thomas Fetterlock was thus able to buy and sell wool grown by other traders and produce and market his own as well. Naturally, Nicholas Fetterlock was being groomed to take over this empire. However, there were schemers plotting to make the business fall into their hands long before Nicholas ever succeeded his father. Into this situation Izzy made his first venture in his quest for insight into and understanding of the past.

The students that had been programmed for the two-week session on this stage of the journey were in possession of copies of *The Woolpack*, which they were required to read at home. (A synopsis of the story was also provided to further stimulate their interest.) During this period of reading, they were concurrently involved in creative and factual assignments from the worksheet that the teacher responsible for this title had prepared for them.

Much discussion, consideration, and comment was of course undertaken in class during this reading-and-writing process. More gratifying, over the whole period of the project's duration, the school corridors, playground, dining room, and routes home became alive with debate over the intricacies of the continuing adventures of Izzy Moonshine. Everybody had a point of view, a perspective, and an opinion to share, and the question, "What's happening to Izzy now?" was frequently heard. The excitement of being involved with the "action" of the peer group was enough to motivate even the most reluctant reader.

Izzy's Second Adventure: The World of "The Iron Lily" by Barbara Willard

On the completion of his first adventure, Izzy's next visit was to Sussex in the sixteenth century, an area still covered in thick and dark forest land. In this place and time, people were naturally suspicious of strangers, the more so now that a war with Spain was looming nearer. The industry of the forest—producing iron in foundries whose huge forges were fired by the timber surrounding them—was booming to supply armaments for the anticipated conflict, and rumors were rife that Spanish spies were at large, seeking to sabotage the British war effort.

On a dark woodland path in the depth of these forests, Izzy encountered a youth anxiously leading a lame horse. The boy, Robin

Forstal, was the son of the local foundry master and had been hurrying home in answer to an urgent call when his horse went lame on the uneven ground. [An overhead projector illustration is provided for the students.] Robin agreed to change places with Izzy, who was soon to learn that the boy's father was dying under horrific and mysterious circumstances.

The chart on p. 83 shows a typical outline of work covered during a two-week cycle on one of the novels, in this case, *The Iron Lily*.

Izzy's Third Adventure: The World of "Whistling Clough" by Walter Unsworth

Having accomplished his study and adventure in the 1500s, Izzy moved on to the eighteenth century and the bleak Derbyshire lead mining moors of this period.

Nightfall was fast approaching as Izzy stepped from his craft, and it required no experience with the geography of England at this time to realize that this was not a friendly place in which to contemplate spending the night. However, while still involved in these thoughts, he became aware of two sensations: the sound of a horse threading its way towards him through the rock-strewn undergrowth and the smell of a wood fire, the smoke from which he soon saw curling upwards from another direction.

On stepping from the protective shadows of a large boulder to accost the person on the horse, Izzy immediately found a pistol levelled at his forehead. He introduced himself to the rider, who said his name was Brett Assheton. Brett warned Izzy to be suspicious of strangers in this part of the world [an overhead projector illustration is provided for the students] and explained that he was riding to the home of his uncle, a local sheep farmer and the owner of a lead mine. Brett had been banished to work for his uncle in Derbyshire by his father, a prosperous Warrington merchant, because he had been expelled from his upper-class school for fighting and poaching. Brett readily agreed to change places with Izzy, and, on finally parting with his pistols and accepting Izzy's gold, he directed Izzy in the direction from which the wood smoke was drifting, warning him to be on his guard.

Izzy proceeded to make his initial encounter with Black Jake, sheep stealer and owner of the camp fire. Izzy daringly extracted half a guinea from Jake for the price of the sheep Jake had stolen from the farm Izzy was now headed towards. The owner of that farm, Izzy had learned, was far from prospering.

The Iron Lily

Typical Outline of Work Covered during a Two-Week Cycle

Week 1

Week 1 includes creative work based upon ideas presented in the book. The first lesson is an expansion of the plot and the setting of the story, and each pupil is presented with a synopsis of the content.

Work Set

The following questions are given to the students.

1. On the death of her husband, Robin's mother persuades the iron workers to move with her deeper into the forest to set up a new and more profitable foundry. You are one of her workers. Describe why you decide to go and what you feel and experience on the journey.

2. The foresters are suspicious of strangers and will not work for them. Robin's mother employs other strangers who are suspected of being Spaniards (religious enemies). The foresters march on the foundry, and Izzy is sent for help. (The incident on which this is based takes place on pp. 100–1 of *The Iron Lily*.) Imagine you are Izzy on this ride. Describe your sensations and emotions (in poetic form). How do you persuade virtual strangers (your neighbours) to help you?

3. The Confrontation: Robin's mother, her workers, and the neighbouring iron master's workers versus the foresters (incident described on pp. 104–7 of *The Iron Lily*).

   Imagine you are Robin's mother. Make your case.

   Imagine you are the leader of the foresters. Make your case.

   Imagine you are one of the Welsh strangers. Make your case.

   Imagine you are the neighbouring foundry master. How do you react to this situation?

These perspectives will be compiled into a dramatic representation called "The Confrontation," the conclusion of which will complete the plot of the novel. Robin and Ursula (the neighbour's ward) are married, and their families are united. Pupils receive a description of this new family, as their lifestyles reflect many aspects of sixteenth-century life that are to be worked upon in week 2.

Week 2

During week 2, students do library research into facets of sixteenth-century life that are highlighted in the novel. Topics may include religious convictions, the patronage system, the development of different processes for iron production, etc. Students are then asked to prepare a report on their topic, in the role of Izzy. The report should be something that Izzy could present to the New People upon his return to his own time.

Izzy's Fourth Adventure: The World of "The Nipper" by Catherine Cookson

On leaving the eighteenth century, Izzy travelled to the coal mining areas of England's Northeast in the nineteenth century. As he stepped from his craft into grassland just outside a town, Izzy disturbed a young boy setting wire traps for a rabbit he was hoping to catch. Striking up a conversation with the boy, Izzy learned that the rabbit, if caught, would be the first meat the boy and his mother would have to eat since a week ago, when they were forced to leave the farm where they had been employed. (The farmer employing them had been forced out of business.) The boy pointed to a shabby, broken-down, decrepit building, which Izzy had assumed to be derelict, where he and his mother were now living. Sandy Gillespie, as the boy was called, went on to explain that his only friend in life was a Galloway pony that he had owned on the farm and had been forced to sell as a pit pony. Sandy was to join his friend in working down in the mine on the following day. [An overhead projector illustration is provided for the students.] His only encouragement in the prospect of going into the mine was that he would be able to ensure that the pony was well treated. Sandy explained his dread of working in the mines, in the appalling conditions of the time, and voiced the opinion that he would probably only get a few days work, as he had overheard his rough and vicious neighbours planning a strike, one that he doubted they would conduct in a gentlemanly and passive manner. You will no doubt imagine how readily he agreed to exchange roles with Izzy for the period of the study.

Izzy's Fifth Adventure: The World of "The Incline" by William Mayne

Izzy's final visit to the past took him to the twentieth century, to a Northern stone quarry in England in the late 1920s. Approaching the quarry from the outskirts of town, Izzy was immediately impressed by the sight of the huge iron wheel at the head of the quarry and by the railway tracks carrying lines of empty and full trucks from the quarry to the town and back again.

Near the bottom of the hill, no great distance ahead of him, Izzy spotted a youth his own age, uncomfortably dressed in a stiff collar and well-pressed suit, who was preparing to jump aboard an empty truck and thereby hitch a ride to the head of the hill. Sprinting forward, Izzy managed, in the nick of time, to jump aboard the same truck and breathlessly introduce himself. The youth was Mason Ross, son of the quarry foreman and overseer, who was just returning from his first day's work as a banker. [An overhead projector illustration is provided for the students.] Mason explained that his father's overseeing role as a foreman stemmed from a serious quarry injury which caused him to lose the use of an arm. Having seen the advantages of an administrative job and not wishing to risk his son's becoming incapacitated striving to achieve it, Mr. Ross had insisted that upon leaving school his son join the ranks of business rather than working people.

Mason further explained that the bank to which he was apprenticed and the quarry that his father administered were owned by one Jedediah Spitalhouse. Jedediah came from the same stock as Mason's family and was brought up with Mason's father, but his business brain, dynamism, and foresight for expansion had led him to control the most sizeable business empire in the area, which now employed most of the town's inhabitants in one way or another.

Having persuaded Mason to change places with him, Izzy continued up the railway track to the Ross home. However, upon arriving, he learned that a significant piece of machinery had exploded in the quarry, nearly killing one of the workers. Consequently, the quarry had to be closed down until the machine was repaired, and Mr. Ross was being blamed for the absence of parts and funds which had precipitated this situation.

Upon accomplishing the purpose of his final journey through time, Izzy returned home. His records of the achievements and adversities of the past were tabulated and people of the future never failed to remember and reflect upon the debts they owed their ancestors.

What Does Izzy Achieve in Educational Terms?

I conclude this chapter with my judgments about this project's benefits to students and its possible extension.

1. Izzy's story provides a framework for reading interest which shows that each novel offers an imaginative world well worth visiting.

2. The story offers initial criteria for the comparisons that are the stuff that criticism is made of at this stage of intellectual development. "Which fictional worlds did Izzy find easiest to enter and why?" "Where did he learn most about the human nature he sought to understand?"

3. Izzy's journey opens up possibilities for historical and geographical extensions as well as literary ones; for oral, dramatic representations as well as written ones. It also opens up excellent opportunities for pupil-to-pupil interaction. It is possible to have a team of teachers who each teach a particular novel, but an alternative way of working is to have one teacher and a whole class working on all the novels. Groups of pupils can then identify what for them are the most significant questions and pass those questions on to other groups for discussion. The value of explanatory talk between pupils can hardly be exaggerated. Of course, the teacher will join such talk (without dominating) whenever possible.

4. Izzy's adventures make pupils aware of the distinction between imaginative and informative writing and provide, through the inspiration of the text used, a multitude of evocative extensions for either mode.

5. The recording of pupils' experiences in relation to their travels is relatively simple. They merely keep a diary of their reading routes (and associated experiences and perspectives) written up in the detail that is appropriate for a particular child at a particular time.

What Do Pupils Think of Izzy?

Extracts from learning logs that pupils kept during the "journey" to record their impressions make the most powerful statements about the real learning through empathy that this project engendered. Pupils wrote:

> I don't feel like I am studying a book, I feel like I am part of it.
>
> Why can't we always go on a journey like this, it makes everything make sense.
>
> Lots of times when I read books I think, "Why did they do that?" But now that I'm Izzy I always seem to get the right answers.
>
> I know I'm learning a lot about history and why things happened but I don't seem to be having to think about it.

Where Does Izzy Journey Next?

The tight simplicity of the initial structuring of the project makes it comparatively easy to extend this approach to other novels by having pupils invent their own time travellers and criteria for period choice. The doors of historical and futuristic fiction are wide open for the further adventures of Izzy Moonshine, or for Izzy's son or daughter. Some suggested titles: *Altar of the Ice Valley, The Lothian Run, Eusebius the Phoenician, The Golden Goblet, The Emperor's Winding Sheet, Spanish Letters, The Namesake, Warrior Scarlet, The Luck of Troy, Custer's Gold, Miss Rivers and Miss Bridges,* and *Aidan and the Strollers* (all Penguin/Puffin titles). A collection of titles such as these can be quickly selected from any publisher of quality children's literature.

Another natural development is the exploration of other writings by authors involved in Izzy's journey. Barbara Willard and William Mayne, in particular, provoke curiosity as to their other novels. For pupils to read individually and then to "present" specific episodes from such novels proves to be an effective way of widening interest.

II Compromise and Redefinition: Reader Response and the Analytic Method

7 Response Model and Formal Method in Tension

Derrick Sharp
Uplands, Swansea, Wales

Derrick Sharp returns us to a formal definition of the response approach and contrasts it with the more traditional method of English instruction prevalent in Wales. Like Dixon, Stratta, and Dias, he shows the consequences of commonplace institutional practices and societal expectations on a response-centered curriculum. These restraints include the Welsh legacy of university literature courses, public exams, bilingualism, the trust in education for social mobility, and the constraints on the teacher's daily choices about how to teach. His observations are undergirded by two surveys into Welsh methods of teaching English. As both practical realist and theoretical idealist, he suggests a genuine combination of the best features of both.

The Cultural Context for Literature Instruction in Wales

The contrasting claims of the personal-response model and the traditional formal method, found in various forms throughout the English-speaking world, are clearly demonstrated in the range of practice in the teaching of English literature in Wales. The Welsh have a high regard for education, largely because historically it offered the academically able an escape route from the industrial rut, especially the coal mines. And education offered a means of escape most often when it was provided to the previous generation as well. As a result, traditional attitudes and expectations have a marked effect on the educational system in Wales. A strong tendency to be formal and traditional in teaching methods characterizes instruction. On the other hand, there has been considerable development and progress in all aspects of education during the last twenty years or so, especially with the advent of comprehensive secondary schools. In the field of teaching methods, therefore, there is a conflict between

91

the old and the new; in the teaching of English literature, between the formal approach and the response model.

The teaching of English literature in Wales is, of course, further complicated by the use of two languages in the principality. It is generally agreed that all the advantages and disadvantages of bilingualism can be studied in the context of Wales, and the teaching of English literature is no exception. Latest estimates suggest that about 11 percent of students have Welsh as their first language, and these are concentrated mainly, but not exclusively, in bilingual communities such as the county of Gwynedd in the northwest. In the bilingual areas, the teaching of English literature is not affected to any great extent after the age of thirteen. The learning of the English language by pre–thirteen year olds, however, is marked by a slower rate of development for Welsh first-language students who require special attention to the differences in English spelling and syntax, for example. The effect of language study on the study of English literature is obvious:

> For all Welsh first language pupils, however, concentration on fluency, command of idiom and mastery of various registers must continue throughout the secondary school, for it is in those language areas that they are likely to develop less rapidly and surely than English first language pupils. . . . The problems are severe for a minority of Welsh first language pupils, those whose command of reading and writing in Welsh is limited or severely retarded. (Sharp, Bennett, and Treharne 1977, 14)

These language areas mentioned are those which are most needed in order to respond to the subtleties of literature. Literature study is further complicated by the insoluble problem of finding enough time for both oral and written work in both languages. It is not necessary, however, to examine these complicating factors at greater length, except to state that two crucial considerations in devising a language policy for a bilingual community are timing and balance.

Bilingual students of English literature in Wales do enjoy two advantages despite their problems: they are able to encounter a wider range of literature in Welsh and English, and they can appreciate the particular contribution of Anglo-Welsh literature. Unfortunately, there is a limited amount of Welsh literature available for the early teenage student, and at about this age the student is more attracted by the wealth of suitable literature in English, but the advantage of bringing the approaches of two cultures to the study of English literature remains in most cases.

In the schools of Wales it is possible to find a wide range of ways of teaching English literature, irrespective of the linguistic background of the area. Indeed, the range in one large secondary school may be considerable, in spite of the influences which tend to integrate the work of a department (e.g., the syllabus and departmental discussions). It is impossible to paint a clear picture of the whole situation in the field of English literature because there are few statistics and the references are usually those which are common to the teaching of English literature in England and elsewhere. We must rely on occasional surveys, such as the one described later, and the informed opinion of teachers, local education-authority advisers, Her Majesty's Inspectors, and research workers. However objective these sources may be, they are bound to reflect tendencies and trends rather than firm evidence. Neither can we measure the quality of the teacher, which may well determine the success or failure of any particular method, traditional or progressive.

The Traditional Model in Wales

Bearing these reservations in mind, we can start our examination of the formal method and the response model by making a crude distinction between the two approaches. In practice, and especially with less capable teachers, the formal method places an emphasis on the handing over of knowledge; it concentrates on the factual aspects of literature. In contrast, the response model emphasizes the students' responses to literature and learning, rather than teaching. The response model involves teaching, of course, but of a different kind. There is usually a higher level of class involvement, too. In Wales, as in England, it is rare to find extreme forms of either method. There are still horror stories of Welsh middle and secondary students counting figures of speech, on the one hand, and reading poems one after the other without discussion or any other activity ("to avoid spoiling the impact"), on the other.

Furthermore, the formal method of teaching English literature deals with form, just as the formal teaching of English language includes a large element of grammer. There is a traditional emphasis on the definition of figures of speech, for example, and their identification in the works of literature being studied. There is a similar concern with structure or plot and other aspects of literature which can be clearly tabulated and learned by heart. These aspects are important, of course, but only as means to an end, as the basis for the appreciation of literature. Formal teaching of English literature may be characterized by the use of study guides or dictated notes and by homework which requires the student to explain the content or subject matter of a work of literature (e.g., a summary of the plot of *Julius Caesar*, scene by scene). Normally the students are expected to accept the teacher's assessment of literary quality and meaning and to conform to conventional opinion, especially in preparation for public examinations, rather than to develop their own response to and appreciation of literature. Often they acquire knowledge about literature, including knowledge of the author's life and other background information, relevant or not, rather than knowledge of literature in terms of first-hand experience; so much so that it is frequently claimed that it is possible for a student to gain a good grade in English literature at Ordinary Level of the General Certificate of Education without any appreciation of literature at all. Extremists even claim that appreciation of literature is a handicap in this examination.

What are the origins of the formal method of teaching English literature? Perhaps they will throw further light on the method. The key is the other term often applied to this approach—*traditional*. In many university schools of English the "knowledge about" method has prevailed, usually in the mistaken quest for a body of knowledge that would justify the study of English literature as a discipline. Specialist teachers of English literature have been trained in these university schools and have been, and still are, influential in imposing a formal method as the only academically respectable approach for all students. Thus we often see an analytical method for in-depth study of a limited but representative sample of English literature; this is the traditional method. Wide reading without a basis of analytical study is not recommended, even for those who can hardly read at all, but who can certainly respond to literature on television. Another contributory factor from the history of English literature teaching is the large classes (often between sixty and seventy students) that were common in English and Welsh schools at the turn of the century. No teacher, however inspired, can deal with the individual responses of sixty students in one lesson. The only viable method is rote learning and chanting, a particular type of the formal method which has been modified into the contemporary approach.

Research on Teacher Styles in Wales

Some form of the traditional method, in many cases combined with one or more elements of the response model, is preferred by the majority of those who teach English literature in the schools of Wales. This emerged quite clearly during the work of the Schools Council Research and Development Project on the Teaching and Learning of English in Wales, 8–13 (1973–77). Of the five surveys carried out by the project team, the relevant one here is that on methods of teaching English. The results of all surveys, which reveal tendencies and trends, it should be remembered, were produced in mimeograph form and circulated to local authorities and colleges throughout Wales, but were not published in any wider sense. The methods-of-teaching-English survey was conducted by questionnaire more than ten years ago, but informed opinion would suggest that the results would not be significantly different today. If anything, pressures since 1974 would tend to make teachers more formal than they were then. What follows is a summary of the salient features of the survey, which was conducted in two parts. The first part was a questionnaire completed by 166 teachers: 121 from junior schools (ages eight through eleven) and 45 from secondary schools (ages eleven through thirteen). Only 12 had more than 25 percent Welsh first-language students. The second part was a personal interview along the same lines with 86 teachers in predominantly Welsh-speaking areas: 36 from junior schools and 7 from secondary schools.

Replies to individual questions showed that only 15 junior and 10 secondary teachers gave more than half their lesson time to oral work: that 22 junior and 19 secondary teachers required their students to write extensively less than once a week; that comprehension exercises were used by all teachers except one, but that the material was rarely worthwhile reading and that few questions tested response as well as literal understanding; that only 28 junior and 21 secondary teachers gave *regular* drama work; and that only 49 junior and 2 secondary teachers *regularly* used small groups in their English lessons. The general picture was one of the retention of formal elements even in otherwise progressive classrooms. Support for the general picture came from the emphasis on accuracy and formal work, or at least on a balance between formal and informal, in replies to the final, open-ended question.

The personal interviews with 86 teachers in predominantly Welsh-speaking areas revealed a similar pattern. The English teaching practice of 26 percent of them showed a balance between formal and informal elements; 65 percent gave more emphasis to the formal elements; and only 9 percent were on the informal side of the "neutral" band. There are many very small primary schools in the predominantly Welsh-speaking areas, and it may be that formal methods, such as exercises and working through a graded series of texts, are seen as the solution to the problem of four age groups with one teacher. But in all areas there was a feeling, partially expressed, that formal study of literature is work and therefore the proper concern of school, whereas talking and acting are "play." The Puritan tradition in Wales lends its support to formal methods.

The general emphasis on the retention of formal, traditional approaches shown by the project survey compares with the similar findings of the more rigorous Bullock survey (Bullock 1975). Informed opinion provides further support on the precise topic of the teaching of literature in secondary schools:

> English and Welsh courses in some schools confine their attention to a narrow range of set books and both during and after the examination year treat the poems, plays and stories as texts for annotation, summary and inappropriately sophisticated explanation. In such situations adequate attention is not given to encouraging personal insight, to enabling pupils to realise the connection between their responses to living and their responses to literature. (Welsh Office 1979, 17)

Constraints against the Response Approach

Discussion with teachers indicates that the legacy in schools from the academic study of literature is a strong influence on methodology, reinforced in some cases by the feeling that good literature, however defined, is wasted on the less academically able students. Fortunately, the influence of both these ideas has declined and continues to decline as the secondary school system becomes more and more truly comprehensive. The other influential factor remains as strong as ever, however. Many teachers of English literature in secondary schools allow their courses to be dominated by the public examinations at the age of sixteen-plus, so much so that the fear of poor results leads them to cling to what they see as the tried and tested traditional methods. In defense of traditional practice, the arguments are often circular, and the circle becomes vicious when teachers are determined to teach as they were taught, unaffected by progressive ideas encountered in their initial training. The many good teachers are always an exception, and we are, of course, dealing with shades of grey, rather than black or white.

The conflict, both theoretical and practical, between the formal method and the response model, is thus seen not only in general terms but also at the individual level, when teachers decide on their approach to the teaching of English literature and as they reconsider their practice from time to time. They are under pressure from more progressive ideas in initial and inservice training, further promoted by local education-authority advisers and Her Majesty's Inspectors. And though the majority in Wales resist this pressure to a considerable extent, as we have seen, the response model is making slow but steady progress, most often in the acceptance of a few elements at a time rather than a wholesale acceptance. We shall look at this kind of mixed approach later, but first let us indicate the salient features of the response model in Wales.

The Response Model

The model emphasizes the students' responses to the individual work of literature and stresses their learning as much as the teacher's contribution. The students are more actively involved in the process, and the focus is equally on the student and the literature, rather than essentially and almost exclusively on the literature, as in the formal method. The transmission of knowledge becomes a means to an end and not an end in itself. Over time, the intention is that students will come to an appreciation of literature, to the best of their abilities, and that at all times they will enjoy literature. In the classroom there are realistic limitations on the extent to which this can be achieved, but the aim remains.

There are clear, basic principles of the response approach, some of which include:

1. Literature is for *enjoyment*.

2. The teacher must also be concerned with the student's developing *response* and the expression of it in speech and writing.

3. The first consideration in the choice of reading is the involvement of the students. Any reasonable literature may be used as a starting point.

4. A literary critical approach is not appropriate before the fourth secondary year (approximately age 15), and then only in simplified form with academic streams.

5. Plenty of books must be readily available if we are to succeed in encouraging reading.

6. Reading fiction must never be replaced in the primary school by reading for information. A balanced programme is required.

7. Shared experiences with literature are a valuable part of development. Group or whole-class reading and discussion of the same book should be part of our work.

8. Poetry should be included at all stages. Poetry writing should be encouraged but not forced.

9. Free or spontaneous drama with younger children should continue into the secondary school, developing into scripted drama for many and theatre for some.

(Sharp 1980, 78–79)

This selected list of basic principles shows clearly some of the essential differences between the response model and the formal method of teaching English literature. It also explains the tension that may arise when the two approaches are in conflict, either in the mind of an individual teacher or in the opinions of different teachers in a primary or secondary school English department. One source of difficulty is often the prominence given to the student's opinion in the response model. We may throw more light on the situation by looking in detail at some aspects of the freer approach to literature teaching.

Of fundamental importance to the response model is the development of good oral work. This does not mean only the set-piece oral lesson, such as prepared talks and reading aloud, though these have their place. Above all, it means recognition of talk as a vital part of the learning process. In the course of talk, student-to-teacher and student-to-student, there is a process of clarification of ideas and opinions. Students strive to grasp concepts and then use their available vocabulary in mutual- and self-correction to remove ambiguity or incoherence, to consolidate their points, and to fix ideas, perhaps in a single word or phrase. Discussion of the work in hand should occupy a prominent place in all lessons, but it is particularly crucial in literature lessons in order that the development, refinement, and precise expression of students' responses may be encouraged at all times. Formal, traditional methods tend to see a silent class as a good, hard-working group, and a preponderance of oral work as a recipe for indiscipline or even anarchy. The response model demands a great deal of talk so that the model may work, and it would be foolish to suggest that this kind of "learning talk" can be switched on at will. It takes a great amount of time and trouble to achieve it, but it is vital. The teacher's task is to provide the learning environment, to plan a series of varied experiences, including the very important development of relationships, a process that can be illuminated and enhanced by the study and discussion of literature. The Bullock committee (1975, 67) saw the teacher's role as planned intervention in the child's language development. It should be clear by now that the teacher's function in literature work is the same— planned intervention, guidance, and encouragement. This is much more demanding than most procedures in the formal method.

If we consider the teaching of prose literature, we find equally marked differences in emphasis between the response model and formal methods. In the primary school, the emphasis must be on enjoyment of and response to fiction. For less-able students in the secondary school, the process should continue in this way, the emphasis remaining on enjoyment and on developing response, usually expressed orally.

> There can be no question of formal study of literature for these pupils, but they can be encouraged to talk about the story (or plot) and the characters (in terms of people they know). For pupils of average or above average ability, the approach in the early secondary years is essentially the same—enjoyment and discussion of plot and characters—but there will be a more rapid development of the expression of response, though it may be no more deeply felt. Superficial interest is of more importance for the less able or reluctant, while books for study by academic classes must be capable of standing up to comparatively rigorous examination. (Sharp 1980, 64)

Some argue that formal methods actually produce reluctant readers. So often traditional literature lessons are based on unsuitable texts studied in ways that lead to boredom and that create students who leave school determined never to read a "good" book again. This is bad teaching, anyway. In contrast, the response model promises at least a chance that students will acquire the reading habit. Much depends on earlier work in the primary school, where the teaching of reading sometimes stops short at the level of mechanical mastery instead of going on to develop the kind of reading which forms the basis of literature studies—emotional response.

Particular Methods within the Response Approach

One particular approach to the study of the novel that illustrates the essence of the response model is that described by Stratta, Dixon, and Wilkinson (1973). They advocate "imaginative re-creation," which concentrates on the student's responses in the form of re-creating the experience of the novelist to the extent that the student may develop part of the novel in a variety of ways. This re-creation may include changing the author's viewpoint, rewriting in another context, writing a television or film version, or translating single chapters or incidents from the novel into drama.

In drama instruction, the contrast between traditional approaches and the response model is equally clear, for the former concentrates on scripted drama while the latter advocates the use of dramatic activity (free, spontaneous drama—learning by doing) as part of a continuous development that leads eventually to scripted drama (and, for some, to the academic study of plays).

> For many secondary schools, drama has traditionally meant the reading of dramatic literature with, perhaps, performances of a school play. The expansion of this attitude to include many of the activities found so rewarding in junior schools has been a welcome change. Drama no longer consists of static play-reading at the desk with a few chosen readers and the rest of the class passive listeners. Dramatic activity can and should include mime, group-work, discussion of interpretation and presentation, production design and set construction, prop provision and music selection. . . . Not all pupils wish to be or are gifted to be performers but all can be participants in the adventure. (Sharp, Bennett, and Treharne 1977, 96)

Response is achieved by active involvement, and in this way we can cover both educational drama (or free or spontaneous drama) and scripted drama (and drama as literature and possible theatre) at the appropriate stages.

The response model of teaching English literature has certain advantages, it can be argued, which may be summed up as follows:

1. Learning by talking and developing responses to literature leads to a firmer grasp of the works studied than does rote learning or the regurgitation of someone else's notes.

2. There is an emphasis on personal development, especially emotional development, which leads to appreciation of literature as well as of life.

3. The model encourages enjoyment of literature and a proper response to it. There is every hope that classes will not be bored and will not turn against literature.

No doubt some readers will add to these advantages, while the formal-method champions will put forward counterarguments.

Mixing the Response and Formal Approaches

The survey reported earlier (that done by the Schools Council) indicated a continuum of methods from the formal extreme to the free-response extreme. Very few teachers in Wales were at either end of the continuum, the majority being on the formal side of the middle or neutral band, and others being spread on both sides of the band. The significance of this is that most teachers adopt a mixture of methods, and it is worth considering what this means in practice. Is there a mixed method which might appeal to a large number of teachers, which could be recommended, which would remove or reduce tension, and which might move the majority from the formal to the response-model side of the continuum? This must be seen against a background which tells us there is no one "right" way of teaching English literature, but which at the same time suggests that an exclusively formal approach does not encourage children to develop a love and an appreciation of literature. A successful mixed method must rest on a foundation of properly devised, balanced activities. Such a balance must include not only the obvious factor of different kinds of literature, for example, but also a balance between the four language skills of listening, talking, reading, and writing. It cannot be stressed too much that balance does not always mean equal attention to, that the initial emphasis on listening and talking will be replaced (though not entirely, of course) by close attention to reading and writing. After these early stages when skills are mastered, there should be no stage when one or another of the four areas is not a vital part of work in literature lessons. Too often formal methods have led to the elimination of talking to any purpose and have exalted passive reception and later regurgitation.

In any mixture of methods there are bound to be elements which are incompatible. We cannot have response in any meaningful sense without talking. We cannot find time for both the rote learning of figures of speech and the development of free response in both speech and writing, and we cannot have enjoyment as the prime aim for all students if we restrict our choice of literature to the nineteenth-century classics. Nor must we allow ourselves to be deceived into thinking that our mixture is good and effective when it contains irreconcilables or when it contains elements that are not properly understood or applied. One example of this may be called the "fake response" model. This apparently encourages response from the students, but, in practice, this response is teacher-dominated, so that in many cases we have a situation in which the students are trying to guess what the teacher wants them to say. All response is conditioned to some extent by the very presence of the teacher, but the students' responses should be free within unavoidable limits, otherwise we are grafting an element of response onto formal methods without proper synthesis. Rather than removing tension, such a procedure increases it for all concerned.

Our aim must be, then, a genuine combination of the best features of both the formal method and the response model. It is worth reminding ourselves that some teachers in Wales have achieved such a mixture, however difficult it may be to define. The best features of the formal method include a framework or structure which provides a sense of direction and a realization of various stages. The danger is that such a framework too easily becomes rigid and is adhered to at all costs. The structure we need must be flexible, so that we may take advantage of the unexpected, brilliant response, instead of rejecting or ignoring it. Flexibility is probably best obtained by a schematic balance of those activities already noted.

Another formal feature of value, provided we remember the safeguards, is the need for a proper basis of fact in our study of literature. Information should never be the sole target of literature lessons, but it is vital to refine response, even in the younger age groups, by constant reference to the text and in this way to avoid theorizing in the abstract. The factual study of literature at the appropriate level is only a first step because, if it dominates, it tends to inhibit response and enjoyment. By the same token, formal work which involves lessons devoted to figures of speech or analysis of the sonnet form without reference to actual texts should be delayed even for the academically able. It should not figure at all in courses for those not academically inclined, although the *effect* of literary devices may be discussed in general terms with classes of any age and ability level. In Wales, the contribution of the formal method must be limited in this way if we are to produce school leavers who enjoy and appreciate English literature.

The advantages of the response model have been listed already. If we postpone or abandon formal work, we can find time for the real response to literature that we want to encourage. But it is only too easy to use the model and produce a course that is essentially chaotic. Planned intervention, including those elements of the formal method described above, is the way to achieve coherence. Within the flexible framework, the teacher ensures that real work is done, that the expression of response is developed and refined, that the class does not simply read a poem, say how good it is, and pass on to the next. Part of the development of response is the growing realization over many years that the answer to "Do you like it?" may not be the same as that to "Do you think it is good?"

Whatever method or combination of methods is adopted, one factor is crucial—the teacher's enthusiasm for literature. This may take many forms, but the temptation to indoctrinate—stronger in the formal approach—must be resisted. The teacher's task is not to hand over ready-made opinions but to develop the student's response. In the response model, properly put into practice, the teacher's response is one among many and, thus, under control though never suppressed. For instance, the enthusiasm may be effectively channeled into reading a personal selection of English literature aloud to the class in installments week by week.

Examinations Drive the Curriculum

Against any possible move along the continuum towards the response model, we must place the pressure of examination, especially public examinations at the age of sixteen-plus. In an ideal world, English literature would not be examined at all, because its most important aspects are extremely difficult if not impossible to assess. In contrast, factual knowledge about literature is easy to test and has, therefore, loomed large in examinations, producing another vicious circle that perpetuates formal methods because the outcome is readily examinable. Much of the tension is reduced, however, when good teaching of the response-model type is seen to offer opportunities for recognition in examinations that employ such techniques as open-book tests and multiple-choice questions and that assign a fair proportion of the marks to course work. The Certificate of Secondary Education (CSE) has done a great deal to eliminate the less-welcome elements of formal examinations, and it is to be hoped that the new sixteen-plus examination, the General Certificate of Secondary Education (GCSE), due to replace both the General Certificate of Education (Ordinary Level) (GCE) and the Certificate of Secondary Education in 1988, will retain the best features of both the older examinations. It is too much to expect that the new GCSE will be less influential than the GCE and CSE in determining teaching methods in English literature, and we must therefore trust that the influence will be more benign. Secondary school teachers often experience conflict between what they know or "feel" to be the right approach to teaching English literature, and what they think, sometimes mistakenly, will ensure good examination results for their students. The GCSE may help to resolve this conflict, even though emotional development, as sponsored by the response model, cannot be easily detected or measured objectively.

Final Tension

The other heartening trend at present is the steady progress made in Wales towards more student involvement of the kind developed in English literature lessons by the response model. Andrew Wilkinson illuminates the important difference when he contrasts a science lesson with a poetry lesson in which the students respond freely.

> The pupils discussing the poem largely determine the direction of the discussion, although the teacher does bring them back to the poem when there is a possibility of the topic being abandoned altogether. Unlike the science lesson, which requires revision of specific material, this lesson allows pupils to initiate their own ideas about the poem, and rely relatively little on direction from the teacher. (1975, 82)

On the other hand, we have the strong pressure on educationalists at all levels exerted by the "back to basics" movement, which places the emphasis on the formal aspects of English, such as spelling and grammar, weaknesses which can be readily detected by the public, especially employers.

> The argument suggests that "bread and butter" English, basic communication at a simple level, is vital in all learning because in this sense it is the medium of instruction and daily commerce. In contrast, "Aesthetic English" concerned with response to and appreciation of literature is an educational frill and can easily be sacrificed on the utilitarian altar. (Sharp 1980, 113)

This argument ignores the crucial importance of learning subtle distinctions among varieties of English in literature and of responding to literature as part of emotional development. Because it is an appealing, apparently logical argument, it increases tension in the minds of the teachers.

The conflict between formal method and response model is present in Wales, and we must work to reduce this impact, not only to help the teacher of English literature, but also to benefit the student. There can be no doubt of the direction in which we should move. Developing response to literature at the appropriate level is a vital part of the student's personal, emotional development. The emphasis must be on the stories, novels, poems, and plays themselves rather than on background, or what is known scathingly as "the hist of Eng lit."

References

Bullock, Sir Alan, Chairman, and the Commission of Enquiry. 1975. *A Language for Life* (The Bullock Report). London: Her Majesty's Stationery Office.

Sharp, Derrick. 1980. *English at School: The Wood and the Trees*. Oxford: Pergamon.

Sharp, Derrick, Gilbert Bennett, and Cyril Treharne. 1977. *English in Wales: A Practical Guide for Teachers*. London: Schools Council.

Stratta, Leslie, John Dixon, and Andrew Wilkinson. 1973. *Patterns of Language*. London: Heinemann Educational.

Welsh Office. 1979. *Literacy and Numeracy and Examination Achievements in Wales: A Further Commentary*. Cardiff: Her Majesty's Stationery Office.

Wilkinson, Andrew. 1975. *Language and Education*. Oxford Studies in Education. Oxford: Oxford University Press.

8 A Developmental Approach to Literature Instruction

Joseph O. Milner
Wake Forest University
Winston-Salem, North Carolina, United States

Joseph Milner answers and amplifies Sharp's call for a combina- tion of the reader-response and formal/traditional approaches to literature instruction. He articulates a four-stage developmental construct for teaching literature which has as its aim the kind of reader Watson envisions: independent and committed. His stages begin with the most fundamental, which is, in essence, the stage of reader response. The next three stages move stu- dents to greater levels of distance from and analysis of the text. He dramatizes what is gained and lost at each of these stages in his account of the teaching of three very capable teachers and scholars.

Over a period of years, I have developed a construct for teaching lit- erature which encourages students to become independent, intel- ligent, and committed readers. The construct is based on principles of cognitive developmental theory. More importantly, it capitalizes on how people most effectively and pleasurably read. Its general movement is from the concrete to the abstract, from immersion in the text to a critical distance from it. In this construct, students' con- sideration of a literary work grows more studied, distant, and com- plex. The construct includes four stages, or levels. As with most de- velopmental theories, one stage is built on the work of the preceding stage and allows for movement into the next.

This relatively simple approach to reading asks students to pro- gress from reader to student to critic to scholar. In the first of the four stages, student as reader, the student is face-to-face with the text; the author's world is unmediated by the teacher's intrusions. In some sense, this is the highest stage of reading, and yet it is often the most neglected in teaching. Students need to be encouraged to surrender themselves to the text; to "receive" the work, not use it;

to allow themselves to be carried into someone else's world first before they begin to evaluate it. To encourage students as readers is to take them back to the basic motive for imaginative literature, the motive which will hopefully draw them back to it when their formal schooling is over, the motive which we might label "entertainment." The teacher's role at this level is to remove scholarly, historical, critical baggage and to free students for their personal journeys into the text.

In the next stage, student as student, I encourage students to reflect on their reading. Many students, of course, read literature only because it is assigned, are uninspired and unchanged by it, and rarely reflect upon it. But even for reluctant readers—certainly for eager readers—questions present themselves that demand to be answered: What happened? Just who are these characters? What does this mean anyway? These elemental questions are the correct ones for beginning to explore the text. Basic questions of event (plot), people (character), and meaning (theme) need to be addressed before more sophisticated formal and critical ones are posed.

In the third stage, student as critic, I encourage my students to take a second step away from the text, to become self-conscious explorers of the "howness" of the literature at hand. The student begins to look at the formal dimensions of the text, to reflect on the author's craft. It is crucial, though, that this stage of formalization be reached only after the earlier stages of enjoyment and conceptualization have been attained. Some students may never move to this stage; their level of abstraction is insufficient; it might destroy their pleasure in reading. Even for a more able reader, such a critical approach is dangerous because it can interfere with the meeting between the reader and the text. Nevertheless, if handled carefully with appropriate students, and after the first two steps are solidly taken, formal matters understood in relationship to meaning can empower the work with new richness. Students can appreciate the literature in much deeper, more nuanced, and more enduring ways.

The final stage, student as scholar, may appear appropriate for an even smaller group of students—those who are sophisticated and have the cognitive capabilities—but I have found it to be freeing and invigorating to students at all levels in the curriculum. At this stage, the teacher invites the student to consider the text with the bias of a scholar from a particular school of literary criticism. Even a simple understanding of the historical, biographical, formalist, feminist, archetypal, or Freudian critical perspective can make students more aware of the total possibilities of the text and the diverse ways in which a work might be understood. The challenge can be energizing and can empower students with a trust in their own imaginative responses.

Table 1 summarizes these four stages in terms of the reader's purpose, primary task, distance from the text, and types of questions about the text.

I formulated this construct as a result of my own teaching and my attempt to help others learn to teach literature, but I never established or participated in what philosophers of science call a "crucial experiment," one which tests the validity or usefulness of the concept. The 1985 National Humanities Faculty Summer Institute at Vassar gave me that opportunity. It allowed me an objective observation of the construct's general merits, which led me to reflect on it and refine it further. The experiment involved the responses of thirty experienced, intelligent, and methodologically aware secondary English teachers to three very capable university teachers and respected scholars: Benjamin DeMott of Amherst College, Alan Craven of the University of Texas, and Harry Levin of Harvard. Each of these "master teachers" explored a literary work with the class: Hardy's "The Slow Nature" and Shakespeare's *Richard II* and *Antony and Cleopatra*. The approach used by each of the three represented a different stage in the continuum: from conceptualization (student as student) to formalization (student as critic) to reconstruction (student as scholar). Each teacher, in his own way, was extremely effective and persuasive, yet each method was incomplete if offered as a solitary approach to classroom instruction. It was notable, too, that each was successively less conscious of or less willing to articulate what he was doing as a teacher. The secondary teachers eagerly reflected upon and argued the worth of each approach; however, the master teachers' discussions of the *how* of their performances diminished in each succeeding session. Descriptions of the three classes may dramatize these three stages and demonstrate the need for their interrelationship.

Conceptualization

Benjamin DeMott was a powerfully vital and dynamic teacher. Though he was the only one of the three who did not explore a play, he was ironically the most dramatic, the one most like a figure on the stage. Moreover, he rendered the classroom exploration of "The Slow Nature" as if it were dramatic action:

Table 1. Four Stages of Reading Literature

Reader's Stages	Purpose in Reading	Primary Task of Reader	Reader's Distance from the Text	Reader's Questions about the Text (Formal Elements and Areas of Study)
1. Reader	Entertainment	Read	Immediate (Unmediated)	*Thatness* Humor/Wit (Sociological) Insight (Psychological) Beauty (Aesthetic)
2. Student	Understanding	Conceptualize	Reflective (Responsive)	*Whatness* Event (Plot) Person (Character) Meaning (Theme)
3. Critic	Appreciation	Formalize	Self-Conscious (Investigative)	*Howness* Form (Structure) Style (Imagery) Intent (Point of View)
4. Scholar	Expansion	Reconstruct	Multi-Conscious (Exploratory)	*Whyness* Context (History) Text (Bibliography) Metatext (Criticism)

Student: She was in shock to hear of her husband's death.
DeMott: Shock? Is that it?
Student: Well, maybe not shock.
DeMott: She must have been in shock when she heard that news.

We watched his classroom, and felt his teaching power as though we were sitting in Amherst reading Hardy.

What he did to us, the way he made us feel the immediacy of the poem, was wholly consonant with his highly conscious, carefully enunciated classroom approach. The term he repeatedly used was *interiority*. It meant getting to the human core of the work. DeMott's objective was to have his students read in such a way as to "animate" the work. He used Emerson's "We animate what we see and see only what we animate" as a way of fixing this as the central activity of teaching. He wanted to focus on the poem's core incidents in such a way as "to take ourselves inside the moment." All of this, he claimed, is our basic role in "serving the poem." What this means for DeMott is staying inside the imaginative experience as long as possible.

In the reconstructed reading of "The Slow Nature," then, he took us to the moment when Kit the joker tells Mistress Damon that her husband John has been killed by a neighbor's cow. Then DeMott continues to explore her response, the depth of her fright as she busies herself with seemingly trivial activity as a way to fly from the emptiness. He wanted us (his students) to pause on that, to experience the impact of that frightening moment as a way of being touched by Hardy's poem. His purpose as a teacher was to train the powers of animation, to sensitize his students to the poem as a "map of feelings." He made it clear that this was his (and our) first and last job with poetry.

He was not naive about the problem or shortcomings of this immediate approach. He admitted that a certain kind of false confidence can arise in students from this kind of teaching, but he preferred that peril to the deadliness of the other approach which anesthetizes rather than animates. When pushed to it, he characterized the literary scholar's baggage as little more than garbage in such a classroom. He did admit that not all poetry is as dramatic as the Hardy piece and that he worked to move students from narrative poems like "The Slow Nature" to more contemplative ones like Shelley's "Ode to the West Wind."

Many of the Institute participants embraced this proposition warmly, but others were less convinced and raised serious questions about all that was left out of this single-minded yet effective way to teach poetry. The recitation of the dramatic action of that Amherst classroom rang true, and the force of DeMott's personality was convincing. He had superbly demonstrated the stage of reading that I have labeled conceptualization. But his basic methodology did not wholly square with the participants' own experiences or ideals for teaching literature. What happened to form? What happened to literary history? Could we not teach our students more?

Formalization

Alan Craven's adroit teaching of *Richard II* answered many of these methodological questions but left still others alive and unattended. His innovative and effective approach to *Richard II* was foreshadowed by an astute question during DeMott's earlier session: "Why does Hardy use the less serious-minded Kit as a strange foil and frame for the central emotional event, Mistress Damon's poignant response?" This question of the author's craft and the response to it point to the next stage of reading, formalization. (In fact, Kit's move from teasing to consternation and back may be the focal moment in the poem or, at least, may reflect Hardy's comment on these events.) The complex formal matters that were intentionally unattended in the earlier session became the focus of Craven's exploration of *Richard II*. Craven was less conscious of his method than DeMott; he was more directly concerned with the participants' exploration of the play than with giving the group a sense of his intentions and success with his students. There were few echoes from his own classroom. His pedagogy was well conceived and somewhat innovative, yet only minimally enunciated.

With skillful prodding and guiding, he set up the basic questions for the group to explore: What are the sources of political authority? What are the uses of rule? He suggested that these could be explored through attention to Shakespeare's use of two formal elements: the drama's point of view and its structure. He made it clear that York does not function as a traditional central character whose weighty actions shift the course of events in the play, but that, nevertheless, he is critical to the work. His significance is substantiated by his being given more lines than any character other than Richard. Craven argues, then, that York serves as Shakespeare's seer, as his view of the moral struggle before him. York can see, according to Craven, the orthodox view of authority, but he also knows the problems associated with it and so must absorb the shocks of removing God's anointed and establishing another to reign in his place.

As a means of letting the group investigate York's response, Craven selected three scenes from the heart of the play in which York must respond to Richard's excesses and weaknesses while he professes his belief in the divine authority of the king. By using short videotaped segments, Craven allowed the participants to experience the dramatic nature of the play, rather than be imprisoned in the text alone. At the same time, he made it clear that viewing only *segmented* sequences avoided another hazard: a visual overload in viewing the *whole* play which compromises close textual analysis and structural investigation. This more selective viewing, according to Craven, cannot be confused by the students with merely watching Indiana Jones.

In the first of the three scenes, we saw York disturbed by the self-centered and petulant rule of the young king but unable to speak directly and honestly to him as does the other uncle, John of Gaunt. In the subsequent scene from Act 3, we saw York at the side of Bolingbroke as he directly challenges the misrule of Richard and begins to make life-and-death decisions that are the rightful province of the king alone. Craven pointed to the hesitancy, tension, and conflict that are demonstrated in York's departure from Bolingbroke, who has made excessive charges against Richard. Craven noted this moment as an index of York's inner qualms in spite of his ultimate allegiance to the strong rule and goodwill of the would-be successor.

Craven's final scene was taken from Act 4, where York officially presides over the momentous rites of divestiture and coronation. Here, again, Craven centered on Shakespeare's use of York's response to explore one of the most heinous acts of civil disobedience a subject could commit. The repeated references by Richard and others to Golgotha, Pilate, and Judas add greater weight to York's already heavily burdened conscience, yet finally do not deter him because he can see the difference between crucifying the king who had "no fault" and deposing a young king who has grown wiser long after the time when he might have been politically redeemed.

Craven, finally, returned to close textual reading and used echoing phrases from the first and last scenes of the play to voice the sharp shifts in the concept of authority and to frame Shakespeare's exploration of York's moral journey.

Not all the water in the rough rude sea
Can wash the balm off from an anointed king.
(3.2.54–55)
With mine own tears I wash away my balm,
With mine own hands, I give away my crown, . . .
(4.1.207–8)

As York watches the shift of power and considers it carefully, Craven asks us to study York to know how Shakespeare wants us to feel about this heady matter.

With the use of point of view, three-part dramatic structuring, and imagery, Craven let us explore dimensions of the play we could not have touched by examining Shakespeare in the more immediate manner we used for Hardy's poem. Clearly, Shakespeare's drama is a longer and more complex piece. Immersing ourselves in it is more difficult and might leave our impressions scattered and unfocused. We had penetrated the play's conceptual center by better understanding its formal dimensions. These formal matters led us toward Shakespeare's intent (his understanding of authority), which was clearly not expressed wholly by either Bolingbroke or Richard.

Although most people were pleased with Craven's masterful means of understanding the play, some still wanted more. They were uneasy about the failure to draw on the Elizabethan world view, the untouched matter of the Globe Theatre's configuration, and critical response to the play. Craven, with a bit of wit, dismissed this impulse by suggesting that the study of the timbers used to construct the famous Elizabethan playhouse was only faintly related to understanding Shakespeare's plays. He went on to say that if anything preceded the study of the work itself, it would have to be a close look at Elizabethan language—the world within, not the milieu without.

Reconstruction

The hope that some teachers still held for a complete consideration of the context that surrounds the play was wholly fulfilled in Levin's extraordinary Shakespearean scholarship. In contrast to DeMott and Craven, he never referred to his method, was in no way conscious of his role as a teacher, and only once entertained the idea of pedagogical appropriateness (whether the play itself, *Antony and Cleopatra*, might be accessible to seventeen-year-old students). He laid out his information before the participants in a formal manner, but without pretense or pedantry.

He began with a plunge into the center of the play: the problem of learning how to die. He pointed then to the basic dichotomies which structure the play: love and war, duty and pleasure, Rome and Alexandria, land and sea. He next moved to the historical treatment of Antony and Cleopatra by Plutarch and other predecessors, the departures Shakespeare chose to incorporate into his play, and the subsequent dramatic interpretations by Dryden, Shaw, and others. He then speculated on the early failure of the text as a production piece, explaining why Dryden's *All for Love* had been favored. Next, he cited the weak reputation of the work, which lasted until the nineteenth century, when Coleridge praised it and placed it among Shakespeare's "wondrous five tragedies." He then began to focus on the structure, which most critics perceived as loose until the metaphysical scholar Wilson Knight recognized its high sophistication. With this massive context set before his audience, Levin began at last to crystallize his argument for the structure of the work by focusing upon the metaphors which give it such "dynamic symmetry." He amassed a host of supporting examples, noting such parallels as Antony's earlier reference to his death, "I will be a bridegroom," and Cleopatra's echo just before her death at a later moment, "Husband I come."

When the learned man finished, there were no questions. Perhaps his authority left too little room for the participants to enter the discussion. But the better explanation for their reticence might be that so much had been said that little could be added. The venerable scholar had taught us all too well.

A Developmental Construct

The discussion which arose after all three scholars had departed immediately centered not on their scholarly insights but on the questions of which method was correct and who had the right approach to literature. The painful answer might have been Levin or DeMott, depending upon which side of the great divide one stood. One might have, on the other hand, selected Craven as the golden mean. But the developmental answer, the one my construct urged upon me, is first DeMott, then Craven, then Levin. Any other order seems foolish; any short circuiting seems suicidal. Those who teach literature can have their cake and eat it, too. First, choose the good texts which have their own power unmediated by us as teacher-priests; then, penetrate the work at ground zero—character and concept; next, help students explore how form informs and reinforces concept; finally, having done this basic work, when there is world enough and time, take the students beyond their own best efforts to locate the meaning and artistry of the text: let them be enlightened by contexts unknown to them and by both wise and foolish criticism so that they can penetrate the work and, at the same time, rise above it and the critics who interpret it.

9 The Humanities in Contemporary Life, or, The Bull That Could Waltz Away

Michael Cooke
Yale University
New Haven, Connecticut, United States

Michael Cooke ends this collection with a broad stroke, a redefinition of the humanities. He starts with basic questions: What do people read? Why do people read? If they read mostly nonfiction, why do we need the humanities? His answer echoes the ideas of a number of other contributors: the humanities are not defined by a narrow body of work, an official canon, but by an attitude of mind and spirit. He believes the humanities should not inculcate obedience to the past but promote freedom, creativity, a sense of participating individually and socially in human powers. In fact, the humanities must meet the incessant challenge to make the canonized manifestations of the human imagination stand up to present inquiry, to connection with current, practical realities. As demonstration of his ideas, he offers an outline for a course for upper-level high school students on the topic of the stranger which embraces a range of subjects and approaches.

Perhaps we'd all agree that a decade ago the humanities stood off in a corner or side alley in relation to American culture. Today it seems more fitting to think of the humanities taking a last-ditch stand, fighting back against the modern world's indifference or attack. On the face of things, this resembles progress. But, by some devious psychic process, I began to visualize the scene as the humanities bull being tormented by assorted experts and taunted by motley spectators. My sympathies, as they would in Spain, rested with the restless bull, and in the freedom of my imagination I would have expected a spectacle of the bull turning the tables on the rest. What flashed into my mind, though, was the picture of the bull stopping its cloudy exertions and waltzing away, as if to say, "Only my bull-necked persistence in this arena keeps these people punishing me (unless I am punishing myself)."

The question before us as humanists today, to my mind, boils down to this: Is there a world beyond our familiar walls, or within them another mode and dimension we have not seen? Despite James Billington's oddly phrased charge that we are "emancipated" from all tradition, we insist on something called "the tradition." The term has become a veritable slogan for us. Its import, however, would seem at odds with sloganeering, as we see if we look back at a couple of notable points in the history of the humanities.

"What [would be] our consolations on this side of the grave . . . ," Shelley asks in his *Defence of Poetry*, "—and what [would be] our aspirations beyond [the grave]—if Poetry did not ascend to bring light and fire from those eternal regions where the owl-winged faculty of calculation dare not ever soar?" For Shelley, hardly more than a century and a half ago, it was not enough to say that no human consolation—whatever eases defeat and grief and pain—and no human aspiration—whatever bends us to new feats, discoveries, to immortality itself—could present itself without poetry. No, for Shelley, poetry was a kind of Prometheus, bringing light and fire to humankind year in and year out, here, and not in some musty old myth.

All we can say is, "You've come a long way, poetry," a staggeringly long way *down*. Thus Arthur Crew Inman in his *Diary* writes poetry off as "artificial chicken food for artificial birds." Put a hundred literate people in a room, and how many would we expect to read poetry? Voluntarily, I mean. Bring together at random one hundred literate academics (the phrase need not be a redundancy), and how many would we expect to read poetry for pleasure? If we divided the world of books, like Gaul, into three parts—poetry,[1] fiction, and nonfiction—and put the hundred at the head of the three aisles, where would most of them go? Into the nonfiction aisle, beyond a doubt. And there they would blithely accept a melange of travel and autobiography, gardening and anthropology, how-to books and medicine, religion and political science and physics and history and economics, mysticism and exercise books and biology. Plus one more subject: technology.

The fact is that, in absolute numbers, more people today are reading poetry and writing poetry than ever before, but *in proportion* to the population, there has occurred a signal falling-off, and the influence on society of those who read and write poetry is approaching nil. "Unacknowledged legislators" are impotent and probably unreal.

Have we changed so much in a brief span (except in Russia, where poetry provides a form of sub-rosa animation and hope and rebellion against the entrenched regime)? I suspect that the people in the nonfiction aisle, people like ourselves, are looking for what people have always held dear: something they can identify with, if only vicariously, like travel and autobiography; something they can learn from, where that learning has some bearing on life (poetry wasn't always above being useful in mnemonic terms); and something stirring, vital, profound, revelatory, like the physicist's account of the origin of the universe or the biologist's accounting for the panda's "thumb." I know mechanics and bailiffs and book-keepers who are excited about Stonehenge and own books on the subject who won't give Wordsworth (who also was excited about Stonehenge) a first look.

It doesn't necessarily get my dander up or my spirits down, then, when a graduate of a distinguished liberal arts college asks me, "Now that we have computers and can fly to the moon and, with technology, can look and listen back for events approaching the very inception of time, why do we need humanities?" My questioner does not truly refer to the humanities, but only to what concretely passed for humanities when he was dosed with them B.T. (Before Technology). He means something like, "Why do we need Wordsworth?" And the answer is that Wordsworth, like Lewis Thomas or Stephen Jay Gould, helps us to come to terms with things that surround us or affect us or attract us, and helps us to come to terms with ourselves in those conditions.

But it is not my purpose to champion Wordsworth, Stonehenge or no. In fact, I find reason to fear the kind of attachment we have to Wordsworth or Socrates or da Vinci or Goethe or Mahler or Picasso or Greco-Roman antiquities. How have we become so entrenched in the habit of identifying the things they present as *the humanities*? Why are we so ready, in the name of *the humanities*, to defend them to the death? Is it possible, for example, that just as Wordsworth and Milton and Socrates were less than popular in their time, we are using them to shut out or belittle our contemporaries, whom the future will see as giants of the humanistic tradition? Should a form or a person that illustrates the humanities end up monopolizing them? Should we see the humanities in particular forms and persons, or with an attitude of mind and spirit? Is the object of the humanities to inculcate obedience to the past, or to promote freedom and fruitfulness and comeliness in the present and the future, drawing as best we can on the past? Perhaps we could profit from Wordworth's attachment to "vital motion," and his warning against a "block or waxen image."

We tend to make the humanities interchangeable with the liberal arts. It should spice up the lives of those who so piously cling to particular forms and persons in the name of the humanities to re-call—here is our second point of history—that the liberal arts in the venerated Renaissance included grammar, logic, and rhetoric (the trivium) and arithmetic, geometry, music, and astronomy (the quad-rivium). Only music, of seven subjects, still has full and ready rec-ognition in our present scheme, and it, with the new synthesizers, seems the most susceptible to the imperialism of technology. Mean-while, grammar seems boring, logic either automatic or cold, and arithmetic, geometry, and astronomy, simply alien. And those who see a cure-all for the humanities in a return to rhetoric only make deliberate what an accident of time has done to our educational structure: they cut off one part, canonize it, and treat this unholy in-jury as the height of health and wholeness.

It is clear that the Renaissance did not divide scientists and hu-manists into two opposing camps (though already we can see Shel-ley doing so, with his eternal values set off against "owl-winged cal-culation"). It needs to be made clear that the world of Galileo and Bacon and Harvey did not fail to make that division out of naîveté or a primitive state of mind. We could harbor such a thought only be-cause we have become the captive of current forms.

The great minds of the Renaissance saw through the seduction of forms to the principle of the liberal arts or the humanities, namely, that people need to go beyond function or skill into a sense of free-dom (hence *liberal* arts), a sense of participating individually and so-cially in human powers: disciplined intelligence, dignity, grace, competence in all the major transactions of the culture. Above all, they had, or fostered, a sense of the relationship of one transaction to another, of one arena to another, of one scale to another. That is why they were not bound to arbitrary distinctions of science and hu-manities.

The principles of language and the mind took them into grammar and logic; the principles of human interaction, into arithmetic and rhetoric. Concern with the structure of the world and with their ex-ploratory freedom of action in it called for geometry and astrono-my,[2] and concern for the structure and fruits of the imagination (as well as reverence for the Greeks) sent them into music.

No doubt there might have been, on this reading, seven times seventy liberal arts. I suspect that the number seven was arrived at semi-mystically, being made up of the trinity and the quaternion and all. But if, rather than looking at the number or at the particulars as such, we consider the meaning and motivation, we can save ourselves from a lot of distress and contention about the humanities today. We are hanging on, as to a magic amulet, to the forms of literature or art or music or history or painting or philosophy or architecture or religious studies. We need to let go and remember that those forms are only ways for us to engage with the major manifestations of the human imagination. And we need to recognize that we truly honor those forms not by blind repetitive genuflection but by testing them afresh against new experience and conditions. No one would be inane enough to want to get rid of "forms." But the humanities need to be seen to exist in certain forms *and* indissolubly in the incessant challenge we make to those forms, as manifestations of the imagination, to stand up to present inquiry, in two distinct ways.

The first of these ways comes with the fact that whatever material we consider, and whatever its point of origin, it continues to be acted upon by the force of time. Darwin changed the way we see Genesis, Marx the way we see Shakespeare or a Gothic cathedral. But then Albert Einstein and Jacques Monod and E. O. Wilson changed the way we see Darwin and Marx. In other words, even as we preserve, we test the material; even as we test, we turn an eye to what may be in the offing. Otherwise, we exert all our energy to protect a jewelry casket without making sure what jewels, if any, are still there.

The second way in which present inquiry challenges the manifestations of the human imagination goes back to the odd assortment of disciplines in the Renaissance's liberal arts. The object was not only to sensitize the students (taking aesthetics to be the antonym of anesthesia), but mainly to empower the students, to bring them what mattered currently, to cultivate in them what would work in a practical way, yes, but more, what would work to save them from mere practicality, mere function. The auto worker who sabotages one unit per hundred, as Studs Terkel indicates, is blindly intimating his freedom from machinery and function, his existence as more than a hand, his place in the scheme of the humanities.

It seems to follow, then, that we must take up subjects and approaches that were undreamt of, or were at best speculative and embryonic, when Dante was great, or Christopher Wren or Cervantes or Caravaggio. (I say nothing of the fact that Cervantes and Caravaggio, revered in the tradition, sought to turn tradition on its head.) If the humanist is a traditionalist, why does it seem scandalous to say computer science should be one of *today's* liberal arts—

or anthropology or evolutionary biology or economics? Because we are creatures of habit masquerading as champions of tradition. Does tradition lodge itself in objects or in a dynamic process of relationship? After all, tradition is a handing down of the known, but also a handing on to an unknown. We have fallen, I fear, into the habit of confusing static forms with living, dynamic principles, illustrations with essences. The people who espouse tradition among us may, on this reading, not be traditional enough.

The very idea of embracing computer science must send an earthquake shudder through the Zona Rosa of the humanistic establishment. Okay, I withdraw it. Even if computer science looks today like the equivalent of geometry or astronomy for the Renaissance. Even if it looks basic to our command of ourselves, our sense of aptitude and grace in today's environment.

Let me go back to what seems to be going on in literature, in the heart of the humanities. Let me go back to nonfiction. What can the humanities do in the area of nonfiction to maintain and fulfill its role *as* the humanities? What should the humanities do? What must the humanities do?

First, we need to give up treating expository prose in strictly utilitarian and, worse, service terms. Our students subconsciously balk at this, and they defeat even the utilitarian purpose by turning the writing of expository prose, wherever they can, into the writing of personal prose (the next best thing to creative writing). Where they can't, it is because we vigilantly prevent them, but then we ourselves find the business of expository prose a tad dreary.

We know, and can do, better. Expository prose has the virtue of being an art with a use, just the kind of art for our times, just the kind of combination that physics, say, lives off with its appeal to basic facts and primary emotions. Our culture is voting for expository prose with its pocket books; I'd say our culture is downright gravitating toward expository prose. And we humanists keep treating expository prose as a sort of pre-humanities offering—or perhaps sub-humanities is the fitting term. This serves neither our students nor our cause.

Let us first, then, recognize not just the continuity but the indissolubility between the art and the utility of prose, and let us teach accordingly. Don't insult, inspire; give even weak students or, better, beginning students—of whatever age—the benefit of good work to deal with. Reduce the *quantity*, not the quality of what they meet.

Then let us recognize the continuity between expository prose as art and the other literary fields, that is, fiction, poetry, and drama.

We have, of course, the habit of opposing expository prose and the so-called creative writing fields. But we overlook that there are more hapless beginners per mile in "creative" than in "expository" writing, even though we use the word "remedial" only in the latter case! We have yet to come to terms with the fact that levels of originality, phrasal and formal power, intellectual depth and emotional weight and even musical finesse in expository writing often compare favorably with the creative. Apart from the fact that in expository writing it is possible to be contested on grounds of accuracy or logic, only shades of difference separate it from the creative. We really are working along a spectrum, where at the meeting point it may be impossible to distinguish the meeting shades, even if small movement in either direction along the spectrum produces a fairly clear difference.

What would this continuity between "expository" and "creative" prose mean in practical terms? I'd like to put before you the outlines of a few courses that look, to my eyes, attractive for students who are "into" literature, and at the same time plausible for more distant or disaffected ones. I can't guarantee that you won't be put in mind of the bull, but at least this bull is *not* confined to one narrow arena. The students, by the way, are older high schoolers or freshmen in college (since I can't grasp the conversion supposed to befall a teenager between June in high school and September in college).

I'd take a topic like the stranger, or change, or the house, with the expectation of catching some primary interest. A course on the stranger would read like this:

Billy Joel	"The Stranger"	popular song
Robert Heinlein	*Stranger in a Strange Land*	science fiction
Albert Camus	*The Stranger*	existentialist novel
Joseph Conrad	"Amy Foster" or *Lord Jim*	modern fiction
New Testament	Parable of the Good Samaritan	parable
Old Testament	Psalm 146	psalm poetry
Mary Shelley	*Frankenstein*	quasi-scientific fiction

Selection(s) from the work of anthropologist Mary Douglas or historian of religion Mircea Eliade

Despite my literary leanings, I've omitted Faulkner's *Light in August*. Though it is uncommonly rich in strangers, it is also uncommonly tough in construction, and younger students taken collectively might resist it on the grounds of economy of time.

My purpose is not to substitute for the box called "tradition" another uninspected box called "variety." Nor is it in my mind to give students a little pleasure (Joel, Heinlein) on the way to the single true goal of ascetical critical rigor (New Testament, Conrad, Faulkner). Billy Joel, in fact, has difficult things to say, things that perhaps the surge and lash of the music tend to drown out. I'd like to see a more reflective, a more inclusive response to rock on *everyone's* part (i.e., not only young people). By the same token, as great as Faulkner may be, or Conrad, the subject of the stranger has dimensions they do not reach, and Joel reaches those. And a Mary Douglas or a Mircea Eliade helps us at once to break the fascination of character and personality in literary study, and helps us to a deeper, more humane sense of the issues underlying character and personality. If students begin by taking to "the stranger" because it feels familiar, they should end more lucidly familiar with the story of how the stranger does not remain in static victimization in our culture, but takes a complex path to participation and reconciliation.

A course on change, in the same vein, would include folktales and Ovid's *Metamorphoses* and Charles Chestnutt's *The Conjure Woman* and Charles Darwin's *On the Origin of Species* (excerpts) and material on political revolution and on St. Paul or Malcolm X and on aging and on rites of passage and on drugs from pre-Conquest Mexico to the post-sixties United States and Raymond Carver's work, especially *Cathedral*, and some history of science, so the students can be protected from the superstition that science is always right and get over their own scientific impatience.

I'd like to leave you to toy with the possibilities of the house, as a topic, and turn again to stress the underlying and undying principles of the humanities, rather than the mere familiar forms or arenas we have, in a sort of cathexis, kept going back to.

Of late we have come dangerously close to identifying the humanities with the making of value judgments, as though the humanities bred the righteous person or the arrogant person or the busybody or the lover of power. But I would think of the humanities as fostering the power to be moved, the power to participate, the power to contribute by virtue of a sense of form, a sense of relationship, a sense of proportion. The humanities foster the judgment that comes from recognizing the scope of an issue and having the patience to be precise in treating it. The humanities foster a respect for accuracy, not in repeating slogans, like the organization that dubs itself "Accuracy in Academia" (AIA), but in the sense of (a) conceiving justly and sensitively the implications and ramifications of social gestures and the world's phenomena; and (b) representing, articulating to our fellows the ever-crystallizing positions we take on things. The humanities foster as well a curiosity about change and growth at macro- and micro-levels of experience, even while cultivating the impulse of individuality meshed with a pride in belonging. The humanities foster appreciation and creativity, a sense of exhilaration and of humility before the manifestations, both personal and collective, spontaneous and structural, of human existence.

Reading and writing, literature plays its part in this extensive project. Literature itself teaches that it plays only a part, and the part it plays must be impaired in proportion as we narrow or rigidify its arena. The world today is not that of the Renaissance and is really light years away from the Greeks, say what we want of our dependence on them. Accordingly, I would be no more inclined to teach the traditional epic in a literature course, keeping the principles of humanities in view, than to teach a course called the literature of practicality, the how-to of the humanities. This latter course would include Ascham's *Toxophilus*, on using bow and arrow; Walton's *The Compleat Angler*, on fishing; DeQuincey's *The Confessions of an English Opium-Eater*, on taking drugs; Thoreau's *Walden*, on living in the woods; Hemingway's *Green Hills of Africa*, on hunting; and Robert Pirsig's *Zen and the Art of Motorcycle Maintenance*. You will say that these are, almost to a tee, fitted into the literary arena. And I say, just so. And I smilingly note they are all expository prose. The boundary, the barricade must be arbitrary. Is it not more than time we let our bull (whether colloquial or papal) waltz free?

Notes

1. For the sake of convenience, drama may stand as a subset hereof. It is obvious that no aisle would be devoted to drama as such; drama is, if anything, worse off than poetry in our time.

2. Nor should we shrink from recalling that this exploratory freedom had a heavy imperialistic overlay. Their freedom can serve as a stimulus but not a model for ours.

Editors

Joseph Milner is chair of the Department of Education at Wake Forest University, director of the North Carolina Writing Project, and a member of the National Humanities Faculty. He also chairs NCTE's International Assembly and is a member of the Executive Committee of NCTE's Conference on English Education. He has served as editor of an affiliate journal and has published critical essays on Stevens and Agee; pedagogical essays in *English Journal, English Education, Children's Literature*, and other journals; and research studies in *Journal of Genetic Psychology*. He has also coedited a collection of essays about children's literature, *Webs and Wardrobes*.

Lucy Morcock Milner has taught English to secondary students in two large public high schools and at the North Carolina Governor's School and has developed curriculum materials and tests for medical students at the Bowman Gray School of Medicine of Wake Forest University. She has written book reviews and articles for a variety of general periodicals and educational journals and coedited a collection of essays about children's literature, *Webs and Wardrobes*.

Contributors

Peter Adams began teaching English in South Australian secondary schools (grades 8–12) in 1976. His four years in a small K–12 rural school gave him the additional experience of teaching children in middle-school and upper-primary grades. His particular interests are in writing and response to literature.

Ben Brunwin divides his time equally between teaching in British and American elementary and junior high schools. He is currently working as a writing specialist for Chesapeake Public Schools (Virginia) and as adjunct professor at Old Dominion University, Norfolk.

Michael Cooke is Housum professor of English at Yale University. He has written *The Romantic Will* and *Acts of Conclusion*, as well as books on Byron and modern black literature. He is now completing a study of writers from other cultures, has written an essay on soccer for *The New Republic*, and has had his poems published by many of America's best poetry reviews.

Patrick Dias is an associate professor in the Department of Secondary Education, McGill University, Montreal, and the director of McGill's Centre for the Study and Teaching of Writing. He has served as a consultant to Quebec's Ministry of Education and is now coordinating an international study of response to poetry. He has published mainly on response to literature and the teaching of writing; recent publications include *Making Sense of Poetry: Patterns in the Process* and *Developing Response to Poetry*.

John Dixon and **Leslie Stratta** first taught together in an inner-city London school. After moving into teacher education, they produced *Patterns of Language*, based on their Winnipeg workshops. *Writing: Narrative—and Beyond* sums up their joint research over the last six years. Both have retired following recent cuts to the education budget. John Dixon is perhaps best known for *Growth through English*, which captures much of the spirit of the Dartmouth Conference. He has recently been awarded an honorary Doctor of Letters degree from the University of New Brunswick.

Robert Probst, now a professor of English education at Georgia State University in Atlanta, formerly taught junior and senior high school English in Maryland and served as supervisor of English for the Norfolk Public Schools in Virginia. Interested in the teaching of both writing and literature, he is author of *Response and Analysis: Teaching Literature in Junior and Senior High School*. He also prepared the literature strand of *New Voices* and has published in such journals as *English Journal*, *The Clearing House*, and *Journal of Reading*. He has worked regularly with the National Council of Teachers of English, where he is now member of the National Conference on Research in English, the Committee on Research, and the Board of Directors of the Adolescent Literature Assembly.

Derrick Sharp was a senior lecturer in education at the University College of Swansea, Wales. He now works part-time as editorial director of Multilingual Matters, Ltd., where he is editor of the *Journal of Multilingual and Multicultural Development* and general editor of the Multilingual Matters series of books.

Ken Watson taught English for nineteen years in secondary schools in New South Wales, the Australian Capital Territory, and England before taking up an appointment at the University of Sydney, where he is now a senior lecturer in language in education. He is the author of *English Teaching in Perspective* and coeditor of *English Teaching from A to Z*. He has also contributed articles on various aspects of teaching to publications in Australia, Britain, Canada, and the United States.